Fire in the Americas

Fire in the Americas
Forging a Revolutionary Agenda

ROGER BURBACH
AND
ORLANDO NÚÑEZ

VERSO
London · New York

First published by Verso 1987
© Roger Burbach, Orlando Núñez
All rights reserved

Verso
UK: 6 Meard Street, London W1V 3HR
USA: 29 West 35th Street, New York, NY 10001 2291

Verso is the imprint of New Left Books

British Library Cataloguing in Publication Data

Burbach, Roger
  Fire in the Americas : forging a
  revolutionary agenda. — (Haymarket
  series).
  1. Radicalism — United States
  2. Radicalism — Latin America
  I. Title II. Núñez, Orlando
  320. 5′3′0973   HN90.R3

US Library of Congress Cataloging in Publication Data

Burbach, Roger.
  Fire in the Americas.

  1. Latin America —Politics and Government—1980–
  2. Radicalism—Latin America—History—20th century.
  3. Radicalism—United States—History—20th century.
  4. Latin America—Social conditions—1945–
  United States—Foreign relations—1945–
  I. Nuñez Soto, Orlando. II. Title.
  F1414.2.B87 1987 980′.03 87–23102

ISBN 0–86091–186–1 (U.S.)
ISBN 0–86091–898–X (pbk. : U.S.)

Typeset by Pentacor Ltd, High Wycombe, Bucks
Printed in Great Britain by Biddles Ltd, Guildford, Surrey

Contents

Foreword by Pablo González Casanova ... ix

Preface to the English Edition ... xiii

Introduction: Towards a Political Renaissance ... 1

1. Revolutionary Practice and Theory in the Americas ... 17
2. Socialism and the Democratic Banner ... 41
3. The Neglected Revolutionary Allies ... 63
4. The Internationalization of Struggle in the Americas ... 80
5. The Challenge of the 1990s ... 94

Notes ... 106

The Haymarket Series

Editors: Mike Davis and Michael Sprinker

The Haymarket Series is a new publishing initiative by Verso offering original studies of politics, history and culture focused on North America. The series presents innovative but representative views from across the American left on a wide range of topics of current and continuing interest to socialists in North America and throughout the world. A century after the first May Day, the American left remains in the shadow of those martyrs whom this series honours and commemorates. The studies in the Haymarket Series testify to the living legacy of activism and political commitment for which they gave up their lives.

Already Published

BLACK AMERICAN POLITICS: From the Washington Marches to Jesse Jackson *by Manning Marable*

PRISONERS OF THE AMERICAN DREAM: Politics and Economy in the History of the US Working Class *by Mike Davis*

MARXISM IN THE USA: Remapping the History of the American Left *by Paul Buhle*

THE YEAR LEFT 1: 1984 US Elections; Politics and Culture in Central America

THE YEAR LEFT 2: Toward a Rainbow Socialism

CORRUPTIONS OF EMPIRE *by Alexander Cockburn*

Forthcoming

THE FINAL FRONTIER: Rise and Fall of the American Rocket State *by Dale Carter*

YOUTH, IDENTITY, POWER: The Chicano Generation *by Carlos Muñoz, Jr.*

THE YEAR LEFT 3: Reshaping the US Left; Popular Struggles of the 1980s

ORIGINS OF THE AMERICAN FAMILY *by Stephanie Coontz*

THE 'FIFTH' CALIFORNIA: Political Economy of a State-Nation *by Mike Davis*

AN INJURY TO ALL: The Decline of US Labor *by Kim Moody*

THE PARADOX OF AMERICAN SOCIAL DEMOCRACY *by Robert Brenner*

Foreword

This book has its place within both the Nicaraguan revolution and a revolution in thought. Without the one, its discourse would be less persuasive and even hard to conceive; without the other – which it does not directly address – its terms and concepts would go astray for want of that rigour and expressive form which are bound up with one of the most profound breaks in the art of thinking. For the revolutionary and progressive thought of our times has three original characteristics: first, it makes the re-examination of concepts into a radical, revolutionary act; second, it does not interpret reality by trying to interpret the classics well, but does retain from them such essential explanatory categories as class and socialism; and third, it grasps contradictions and dialectics not as a logic of history but as a series of struggles whose very movement – in our own as well as other times and places – involves change in concepts, language and practice. In that movement it seeks to unravel the possible and desirable course of the revolution.

In neo-capitalism, any reform in the world was seen as the end of revolution. On the left, thinkers from the social democrats to eurocommunists, have given up for dead the capacity of the revolutionary process to transform the central categories. Thrown onto the defensive, many revolutionaries shut themselves up in ideas and terminology that did not express a changing history. Orthodoxy and heterodoxy became the crucial problem of debates, so that new history, real and concrete, escaped them both. On the other hand, the realization of certain ideals entered into the dialectic of history, and debate became dominated by an old form of thought in which idealism is the overseer that seeks out contradictions between words and deeds, between promises and achievements, between the utopias of revolt and the dramas peculiar to any actual revolt. In this way revolutionary, emancipatory thought ceased to understand and express the dialectic of actual revolutions that have been carried through or remain to be accomplished. Among variants that had their origin in liberalism, nationalism or Marxism, conservative thought took a firm hold of criticism.

In the new stage, amid a great epistemological break, revolutionary thought is not concerned whether, in correctly interpreting the course of history, one is correctly interpreting Marx or Lenin. What counts is whether the course of history is being well interpreted, and as much care as possible is taken that the interpreter knows not only the essence of Marx's and Lenin's theory and method but also the theories and experiences of the masses – of Sandino, Farabundo Marti, and the Indians of Guatemala. The problem is to know the present situation and direction of the movement for liberation. Criticism requires that the new right be divested of what it took away from the new left: the half-completed critique of the frozen old left, of its fossilized language, its deification of Marx and Lenin, its obscuring of the contradictions of real-world socialism, its authoritarianism. But unlike the 'new left', the mainstream of contemporary revolutionary thought – of which this book forms part – recognizes the progressive role of the socialist countries in world history. In Marx and Lenin it respects two great figures of revolution and liberation, who are remembered in a secular mode. It analyses the international and internal struggle of the socialist countries, and the limitations of socialist democracy and the 'new man' that are still found there.

The starting point is not to think in terms of models, nor to take the criticism of one's own or other models as a pretext for not thinking. The aim is to conceptualize the revolution in three main fields: decolonization, democratization and socialism. Class struggle is a strategy, not a faith; anti-imperialism is a historical project, the supreme ideal of a world without colonialism old or new, without capitalism or neo-capitalism, and without authoritarian regimes; a society which, far from disparaging the various currents of humanism, joins them together in an ideological pluralism and a universal dialogue that have to be practised here and now, wherever one finds oneself. Self-criticism is all well and good. But it should not involve the confession of errors or denunciations that place blame on others: it is an invitation to lucid and precise analysis, capable of righting the course of the revolutionary and progressive movements when more effective ways of achieving the aim can be rooted within real or potential mass movements.

The authors of this work are a North American and a Nicaraguan. In the midst of the war that Yankee imperialism is waging against Nicaragua, this small Latin American country, the authors received Nicaragua's highest social-science prize that bears the name of the founder and ideologist of the Sandinista National Liberation Front: Carlos Fonseca. This book, as its title suggests, refers not just to Latin America but to the Americas. And of the various objectives for which progressive forces are fighting, it lays its main emphasis on democracy. In this way it links the struggle of Latin America with that of the North American people, the struggle for democracy with a whole revolutionary process in culture, politics and society. Throughout its pages, workers' struggles south and north of the Rio Bravo are constantly appearing and reappearing as the complements that together will open the gates of the twenty-first century, in an organic articulation that will be ever more necessary. Only then will these struggles assert a democracy which, to be worthy of its name, will be liberatory vis-à-vis imperialism and revolutionary vis-à-vis capitalism and every form of exploitation, oppression and alienation. But such a democracy will also have to be pluralist, representative and electoral, leaving behind the kind of argument that used to slight the values of freedom and formal democracy as merely bourgeois.

'Part and parcel of this struggle,' write Núñez and Burbach, 'is our right as revolutionaries to reflect on and discuss our ideas freely, to tell the world openly who we are and to fight to transform that same world without hypocrisy.' Their book is really the agenda for a debate. Focusing on the problem of political revolution in our time, it defines imperialism and allied dominant classes as the principal enemy and raises the banners of democracy and socialism in a serious and thoughtful way. In a single project the authors recuperate nationalism, internationalism and anti-interventionism, conceived in terms of both Bolivarism and liberation. They pose the need to 'win broad sectors of the population for socialism, as the alternative to capitalism'. At the same time they show that no political movement can triumph in the Americas – whether in the USA or any country of the Caribbean or Latin America – unless the masses are convinced that their basic democratic rights will be taken up and driven forward by the revolutionary movements.

This is a book for discussion and, above all, serious reflection, that will be hard for anyone to pass by in the debates of our time. By systematizing the thought that now runs so deep in the continent, it will help to spread that thought more widely and to draw out the implications for emancipatory action.

Pablo González Casanova
5 April 1987

Preface to the English Edition

Fire in the Americas is an updated version of *Democracia y Revolución*, which was first published in Nicaragua in June, 1987. We wrote the book over a three-year period primarily in Nicaragua, at moments when our other commitments allowed us to be together to pore over various English and Spanish drafts and to consolidate a common framework and political vision. Because we wrote the book in different stages, its chapters constitute separate essays. And as happens with many political works of this nature, the authors feel that some of the ideas presented here must be further developed. Indeed, when we sat down to write the epilogue, we found it virtually impossible to tie up the book, precisely because so many of the themes and ideas lead in many different directions. Thus, what was intended as a conclusion is in many ways an introduction. This is perhaps as it should be, because it is our intention that this book initiate discussion, not end with an artificial closure.

We want this book to serve as a political treatise for people in the developed as well as the underdeveloped world, but we recognize that its political fervor speaks most directly to Latin Americans and Caribbeans who are in the throes of revolutionary struggle. Many readers in the United States and Western Europe may criticize us for painting too optimistic a picture of the revolutionary potential throughout the Americas. Yet we believe that the possibilities for socialism in the United States and Western Europe ultimately can be assessed only by looking at the increasing linkages between social movements and class forces on the different continents of the third world.

The political pessimism that many of us experience in the developed world can be overcome only if we are aware that our struggles are inextricably linked to those of our allies in the third world. Their refusal to accept the dictates of imperialism and its local allies challenges the power of international capitalism and weakens our common enemies. Yet at the same time, our third world brothers and sisters look to us to make our own demands, because their dreams of socialism and democracy are unlikely to be fully attained if we do not achieve these goals for ourselves. This book is an effort to draw the struggles in these two worlds ever more closely together, to bridge the political gap that exists between us and to begin forging a common political vision.

Many, many people have contributed to this book. Above all we wish to acknowledge our debt to the staffs and volunteers who work at the Center for the Study of the Americas (CENSA) in Berkeley, California, and at the Center for the Study of Agrarian Reform (CIERA) in Nicaragua. We have imposed many extra hours of work on them in preparing this manuscript. In particular we would like to thank Glenn Borchardt, Ed Coliannini, Eric Holt Jimenez, Martha Kendall Winnacker, and David Landes in the United States; and Angelica Faune, Syta Fournier, and Amanda Lorio in Nicaragua. Edwige Baluntansky provided special assistance in both Nicaragua and the United States in translating, going over the drafts and making suggestions. We would also like to thank the many 'internationalists' like Bill Bollinger, Amalia Chamorro, Carlos Fernando Chamorro, Patricia Flynn, Xavier Gorostiaga, Marta Harnecker, Daniel Martinez, Joel Rocamora, and Sarah Stewart, who helped us in one way or another to formulate many of the ideas that are in this book. Our thanks to Carmen Diane Deere, Richard Fagen, Jose Luis Caraggio and the Social Science Research Council for arranging a series of seminars in the United States and Nicaragua in 1983 and 1984 that took up some of the themes that are developed in this manuscript. Finally, we would like to thank Mike Davis for helping to arrange the English publication of this book.

Roger Burbach
Orlando Núñez

Introduction: Towards a Political Renaissance

This work owes its existence to the Nicaraguan Revolution. This revolution, carried out by a small nation of less than three million people, is at the cutting edge of contemporary history. Nicaragua is under siege precisely because it represents a profound challenge to the historic hegemony of the United States. The Nicaraguan revolution is inspiring not simply because it is confronting the most powerful imperial state in human history but also because the Sandinista experiment serves as a political beacon for others throughout the Americas and the rest of the world.

Nicaragua's bold defiance demonstrates why it is both possible and imperative for the left to seize the initiative in the Americas. The US empire and the capitalist regimes in much of Latin America and the Caribbean are in crisis, a crisis born of severe economic distortions on a global scale and of the exhaustion of the old political approaches used to contain mass movements. The resurgences of US militarism in the 1980s – the New Cold War and the 'Reagan Doctrine' – are reflections of this crisis. They are attempts to hold back the tide of social change and democratization by marshalling the resources of the empire to maintain an *ancien régime*.

To take the initiative, the left needs to develop a new vision. Many of the old ideas and concepts that have guided us for so long are no longer adequate. In country after country the program of the left is in disarray or out of date. Liberalism, the political philosophy that served the imperial leaders of the post-war world, may be dead, but this can be of no consolation to a left which doesn't know how to appeal to the new mass movements. In the United States it has been the New Right that has seized the ideological initiative. Filling the political vacuum left by liberalism, it has struck at the weak links in the ideological armor of the established socialist societies, accusing them of totalitarianism, of being closed societies that violate the human rights of their own peoples.

To deal with this challenge the revolutionary movements in the Americas need a new political agenda. We need to rethink our old ideas, to understand the limits of the established socialist societies, and above all, to incorporate the needs and aspirations of ordinary people into our political programs. Most importantly, we need to recreate the political energy that animated the 1960s, changing the course of history throughout the Americas. Our crisis is in large part a crisis of the generation that came of age in the 1960s.

The Revolutionary Generation in Latin America

In Latin America the generation of the 1960s was galvanized by the Cuban revolution. The objectives and ideology of the Cuban movement were propounded in the First and Second Declarations of Havana, in the writings and speeches of Che Guevara and Fidel Castro, and in the Tricontinental Declaration. The political ideology of that revolution fused the objectives of national liberation and socialism, and it espoused popular democracy, broad political alliances, and armed struggle with the support of the masses.

In 1967, a French writer, Regis Debray, issued a political manifesto based in part on his generalization of the Cuban experience. Titled *Revolution in the Revolution*, the pamphlet incorporated many of the ideas of the political activists who took up arms against the established regimes in Latin America and it shook the foundations of traditional leftist thought. The old Communist parties were denounced for being complacent and inept. To change the world one had to act boldly. Debray's manual asserted that a small band of revolutionaries, called a *foco*, could take to the mountains, survive against overwhelming military odds, catalyze mass support, and seize political power, thereby changing the course of history.[1]

Today, two decades later, the *foco* theory of revolutionary warfare has been repudiated. Even in the late 1960s, political theorists and some revolutionary leaders pointed out critical flaws in the *foco* approach – its voluntarism, its failure to take into account the concrete political realities that a guerrilla movement faces, and its lack of a strategy for working with the masses in the urban areas.

By 1970 many of the advocates of guerrilla warfare were dead, often having been hunted down by counterinsurgency units trained and armed by the Pentagon. The most renowned practitioner of guerrilla warfare and revolutionary internationalism, Che Guevara, was killed in 1967 in the jungles of Bolivia. Among those who survived, some tried to develop new strategies for guerrilla warfare, and still others embarked on the road of reformist politics. Regis Debray, who was captured and imprisoned in Bolivia, returned to France and turned from revolution to reformism joining the French Socialist party.

The revolutionaries who survived and persevered in Latin America learned much. The defeat in the 1960s of guerrilla movements in Guatemala, Venezuela, Nicaragua, and Brazil, as well as Bolivia, demonstrated that it required much more than a small band of rural guerrillas to overthrow an established order buttressed by the USA. Subsequently, Carlos Marighella in Brazil and the Tupamaros in Uruguay tried to adapt the theory of rural guerrilla warfare to urban conditions, but to no avail.[2] Marighella was killed in the streets of Sao Paulo, while the Tupamaros, despite extraordinary heroism, were broken by the local military and police forces under the direction of US military officials and the CIA.

Then in the early 1970s, electoral advances by popular alliances in Chile, Uruguay and Argentina provided a new opening for revolutionary movements. In each country, revolutionary formations mobilized the urban poor, trade unions and farm laborers, while keeping open or developing the option of armed revolutionary warfare. But these endeavors also failed as brutal military regimes seized power in all three countries, killing or imprisoning many of the leaders and thousands of militants. A long dark night descended on most of Latin America, a night that was not broken until the mass insurrectionary rebellion in Nicaragua and the triumph of the Sandinista National Liberation Front in July 1979.

4

The Generation of the 1960s in the US

Although the radical movements in the United States have been far less developed and have by and large pursued different paths, their fortunes have paralleled the left in Latin America and the Caribbean. In the United States a new generation of political activists was also forged in the 1960s. The Civil Rights movement, the Vietnam War, and the demand for a 'participatory democracy' led to the rise of the New Left, the political generation that broke with liberalism and that also questioned the political formulas of the old Communist parties.

As with the *foco* approach to guerrilla warfare, there was much that was flawed in the approach of the New Left. It too was voluntaristic, it failed to grasp the complexities of US society, and it had no real strategy for organizing a broad popular movement against capitalism or imperialism. And as with their Latin American counterparts, these problems led to the breakup of the 1960s generation into different tendencies: a few groups, such as the Weathermen, decided to carry out a form of guerrilla warfare and armed struggle in the United States; others decided to form new Marxist Leninist parties or to join the old formations like the Communist Party or the Socialist Workers Party; and still others moved in reformist directions, joining the Democratic Party, or investing their energies in anti-war candidates like George McGovern.

By the mid-1970s, the New Left was in disarray. The armed groups, like the Weatherman and the Black Panthers, were completely marginalized and many of their leaders were dead or imprisoned as they came up against the repressive power of the US state. Those who had joined the old communist formations had not succeeded in rejuvenating the parties, while those in the new Marxist-Leninist parties spent much of their time engaged in sectarian debates over who had the 'correct political line'. And those who entered into reformist politics had little to show for their efforts by the 1980s as the Democratic Party leadership moved to the right, abandoning economic liberalism.

What happened? What dashed the high hopes of the generation that came out of the 1960s? Even more importantly, how can we today recapture the dynamism and the vision that infused the social and political upheavals that shook the Americas in the 1960s? There are no easy answers to these questions, nor are there any simple political formulas that we can follow. This essay attempts to grapple with some of the central issues, proposing elements of a new synthesis.

The Crisis of Orthodox Marxism

The ideological crisis of the left is demonstrated by a brief look at the progressive and revolutionary movements in the countries of the two authors – Nicaragua and the United States. Perhaps no two societies in the Americas are so different. In the United States we find today that, after a renaissance of left thought in the 1960s and 1970s, intellectual creativity has lost much of its connection to mass struggle. The small revolutionary parties, be they Trotskyist, pro-Soviet, Maoist, or self-defined independent Marxist-Leninist formations, have no following of any significance. With the partial exception of communities of color, the progressive social movements – the feminists, the gays, the environmentalists, etc. – continue to define themselves largely in terms of the single issues they are struggling for. They have no overarching political banner or philosophy that unites them. To the extent that they express themselves on the national political scene, they adopt the strategy of trying to influence the Democratic Party, a party that is unlikely to respond to the legitimate social demands of these movements as it tries to compete with the New Right for the same political ground.

In Nicaragua political practice and strategy are more advanced than theory. While the orthodox Marxist-Leninist parties have maintained doctrinaire positions and have proven incapable of leading the revolutionary movement, the Sandinista Front, by being particularly adept at forging a political strategy that focused on *anti-Somocismo* and advocated national liberation and participatory democracy as the alternatives, was able to overthrow the Somoza regime and deal a strategic blow to the United States. After the victory, the Front mobilized the population against imperialism and began the building of a new society.

Today within Nicaragua some assert that the revolution is a 'Sandinista' nationalist revolution, others say that Liberation Theology is a major driving force, while the revolutionary leadership itself asserts that this is a 'popular, democratic and anti-imperialist revolution'. This difficulty in definition reflects the general crisis of Marxist theory, a crisis that the leadership of the Sandinista Front recognizes only too well. Old political formulas are no longer viable: this is why the Sandinistas are extremely flexible in defining the process, allowing internal debate and experimentation within the revolution itself to evolve new forms.

The very crisis of orthodox Marxist theory gives the left the opportunity to make a leap forward, to set aside old antiquated beliefs, to enrich contemporary Marxist thought, and to develop a new vision for revolutionary movements. But to do so the left needs to address the interrelated issues of ideology, political strategy and theory. The interaction of these elements both defines and sets the course for a revolutionary movement.

We view ideology as the social cement of any social order – the ideals, values or beliefs that guide a society. To pose an alternative ideology in a given society a revolutionary movement must devlop a comprehensive political strategy. This strategy ought to take into account the prevailing values, the ideals that the movement is struggling for, and the concrete tasks that have to be carried out to confront the existing order. Theory is formulated and developed in the course of a revolutionary process. It emerges out of an awareness of past experiences, the evolution of political strategy, and the principles of the movement.

Today the major challenge is to develop a political strategy and a theoretical approach that can bring together the diverse social movements in the Americas, break down their historic isolation, and challenge the dominant order. It is our belief that by drawing on the political experiences of the diverse societies of the Americas, from Chile and Argentina, to Peru, Nicaragua, Mexico, the United States and Canada, the left can collectively begin to develop the theoretical approaches and strategic priorities that will lead our movements into the twenty-first century.[3]

The Worker-Peasant Alliance and New Social Forces

To link political strategy and theory, it is necessary to locate the 'motor' of the revolutionary process. In the advanced capitalist societies, it is the working class that embodies the basic contradiction between capital and labor. In most underdeveloped countries, however, it has often been the peasantry that constitutes the largest single social force. This reality led Lenin to develop the concept of the worker–peasant alliance as the central axis for revolutionary struggle.

We believe that important transformations have occurred in most societies that make it imperative to expand this system of class alliances. While Marx and Lenin were both aware that other social sectors – especially factions of the petty bourgeoisie – could play a role in the revolutionary process, neither developed a program for their incorporation.

History compels us to broaden revolutionary theory and practice. Diverse political experiences, ranging from the Cuban revolution and the political ferment in the United States in the 1960s, to the May 1968 rebellion in France, and the 1979 Nicaraguan revolution, have made it increasingly clear that the impetus for revolutionary change no longer comes only from Marx's working class or Lenin's worker–peasant alliance. Today a *third* social force comprised of a variety of groups – the middle classes, the intellectuals, the urban poor, the petty bourgeoisie, and the ethnic and social movements – often plays a highly original role in social change.

The fundamental forces that drive capitalism today are still the same as those that Marx described in *Das Kapital*. But the social structures of capitalist societies and their state apparatus are significantly more complex than in the nineteenth century. Exploitation in both developed and underdeveloped capitalist societies has now reached the stage where it affects a wide array of social groups ranging from women and ethnic minorities to youth, Christians, the elderly and the middle classes. In the underdeveloped countries, the rural–urban migration combined with the lack of employment opportunities creates an explosive population of urban poor. All these groups not only experience direct and/or indirect economic exploitation – their entire existence is stunted; fundamental values such as culture, love, pleasure and moral decency are destroyed by capitalism's relentless drive to turn everything into a commodity for profit only.

Capitalism also has now developed its productive forces to the extent that individuals, particularly in the industrialized countries, have the leisure time to search for new experiences and definitions of themselves and society. For the first time in history, people can be liberated in the fundamental sense that Marx spoke of in the *Communist Manifesto*. But as long as capitalism exists, this potential will go unrealized: increased leisure time can lead only to frustration and alienation since capitalism offers nothing except the values of the marketplace, or traditional mores like the patriarchal family and stern religious morality.

The ubiquity of exploitation, combined with new potentials for liberation, have been central in creating a third social force comprised of the middle class intellectuals, progressive Christians, and the social movements (feminists, ethnic and minority movements, gays, etc.). As we will demonstrate in the third chapter, these groups sometimes have a greater potential for sparking a revolutionary process than either the workers or the peasantry. Today they are ripe for a new social vision, a vision that will liberate human nature.

Thus the starting point for any contemporary revolutionary process is the shaping of broad class alliances. The working class remains at the core of this process and the *historic subject** of all popular revolutions. A proletarian, or socialist, project must guide this revolutionary process because it is the only way that a classless society can ultimately be built. No revolution is possible without the working class.

But the remaining classes and sectors – the peasants, the urban masses, the social movements, etc. – are indispensable; and they constitute the *social subject** of all revolutions. It includes the diverse popular sectors, which along with the working class, have driven all the great socialist revolutions in the twentieth century.

A major limitation of orthodox Marxism has been the belief that a revolutionary movement can become hegemonic in a given society without forging these broad political alliances. Many traditional Marxist parties have limited themselves to

---

*By 'historic subject', we mean that the working class is the only class that is destined by history to be the antithesis of capitalism while that system exists. By 'social subject' we mean all those social forces that incorporate themselves into a revolutionary project.

organizing the working class (and the peasantry in some cases), while focusing their ideological attacks on the system of economic exploitation under capitalism. They do not build broad political alliances nor do they offer sophisticated political, economic, social and cultural critiques of capitalism. In a crisis it is difficult for these parties to mobilize a broad popular defense against the repressive powers of the state and imperialism.

Because each society is different, each revolutionary movement has to devise a system of class alliances that best responds to the nature of the society in which the struggle is being carried out. There are no simple formulas. Whether the revolution is dominated by the working class, by a worker-peasant alliance, or by a broad mass front is determined by the social structures of the particular country. What is critical in all cases, however, is the need for a political party, a vanguard, a liberation movement, or a revolutionary bloc of parties to provide leadership in shaping strategy. If this leadership is democratic and represents the interests and needs of the popular sectors while maintaining its commitment to a socialist project, it can raise the political banners and generate the ideological vision that are necessary to carry out a political revolution.*[4]

National Liberation and International Solidarity

Nationalism and internationalism are inextricably combined in national liberation movements. These movements confront a system of domination and exploitation that has been shaped not simply by the local ruling classes but by imperialism as well. In nominally independent countries, imperialism has imposed a system of economic and cultural subordination that has degraded national values. To break this system, a national liberation movement has to reclaim its own resources and values, while constructing a new system of international support and alliances. This process – of merging national and international revolutionary struggles – is central in the advance of today's revolutionary movements.

---

*Here we define 'political revolution' as the seizure of power by a revolutionary movement. The 'social revolution' is the subsequent transformation of society and the effort to build a socialist order.

During the past quarter century solidarity movements and other forms of international support for national liberation movements have grown rapidly, becoming important factors in the balances of power. These movements have undermined and even altered the policies of the imperialist powers. They have broken the old patterns of blind nationalism, and they have created a new arena of struggle that is vital for the success of political revolutions. Here we will call these movements the *fourth force*.

Classical Marxist theory conceived internationalism as an activity of an International of workers' parties. It urged: 'workers of the world unite' in a revolutionary International to break the chains of capitalist domination. These assertions do not enable us to understand the full scope of internationalism today. The solidarity movements are rooted in organizations that are neither political parties nor comprised mainly of workers. They are 'people to people movements' that reflect the general development of international consciousness in both the developed and underdeveloped worlds. They pressure their governments to support just revolutionary causes, and they often provide concrete material assistance. These movements are gaining momentum, they are deeply rooted, and it is impossible to stop them precisely because of their growing mass base.

The growing independence of many third world governments – whether progressive or revolutionary – has also become an obstacle to imperialism in the late twentieth century. Entire third world regions that were once dominated by imperialism have today begun to exercise a certain degree of autonomy. In the Americas, the internationalism of the Cuban revolution, and its ardent support of national liberation movements, constitutued the first building block for the alteration of power relations in the Western Hemisphere. Mexico's refusal in the 1960s to join the US blockade against Cuba opened an important breach in the US-dominated inter-American system. Today, the neutral stance of the Organization of American States vis-a-vis the Nicaraguan revolution reveals that the majority of the Latin American and Caribbean countries are no longer willing to lend themselves uncritically to US interventionist projects. In part, this is a reaction to the broad development of an internationalist and anti-imperialist consciousness that extends from Argentina and Chile to the United States and Canada.

Our contention is that these new internationalist forces, combined with the third force, constitute strategic allies of the workers and peasants in a hemispheric revolution in the late 20th century. In the third and fourth chapters we will look at these emerging social forces in some detail. We will demonstrate why they will be in the forefront of revolutionary change in the Americas and suggest that the key to uniting these two forces with the workers and the peasants is the development of a new political vision whose core is radical democracy.

Demoralization and the Democratic Alternative

Since no revolutionary movement even has come close to seizing power in an advanced capitalist country in the postwar period, the left has drawn its principal hope from the triumph of revolutionary movements in the third world. Each successful political revolution has weakened imperialism, nurtured the development of the fourth force and raised the hope that profound change may be possible even in advanced capitalist societies. But the huge difficulties that each social revolution has had to confront have disappointed hopes for dramatic advances and frequently have led to political demoralization. Social revolution in the third world is beset by economic problems, including imperialist blockades and boycotts, that often cause solidarity activists as well as some Marxist theorists to accuse them of having 'betrayed' their early principles.

On the theoretical plane, those who abandon third world revolutions are often confusing the process of building a new society with the final objective, which is a democratic, egalitarian, socialist society. A social revolution is a difficult, protracted, and ultimately, international struggle to change the material conditions of life and to usher in a new era of political and social freedom. During the course of virtually all social revolutions, intervention by imperialist powers has made this task inestimably more difficult. For new revolutionary societies these challenges all occur at a time when their social and political institutions are weak and when the hegemony of the new political order is not yet firmly established.

While many first world theorists need to realize that no

single third world revolution is going to usher in the socialist ideal, third world revolutionary leaders need to develop a greater theoretical and practical understanding of how to advance democracy in the early stages of the social revolution.

In the second chapter we will attempt to develop the democratic content of socialism by looking at how Marxism has related to the issue of democracy in the past, and by showing how democracy has remained a concept the left pays lip service while failing to incorporate it into political practice. This is also true in the developed countries like the United States where the left has refrained from taking up issues like democracy and patriotism because of the way these values have been manipulated by the ruling class and bourgeois ideologists.

A Common Revolutionary Agenda

In this work we have been guided by the following premises:

- *Political action is central to the process of creating a new vision and a new political order.* This may seem like an obvious assertion, but it deserves to be emphasized because Marxists in Latin America and the United States, especially after the setbacks of the past decade and a half, have tended to focus on analyzing the role that the material or productive forces play in changing the course of history. Many assert that the 'objective conditions' are not propitious for revolutionary change and that there is little they can do until these conditions change. A major limitation of orthodox Marxism has been its tendency to focus on economic structures, while forgetting that a revolution can only be carried out by acting in the political realm.

We are not saying that economic conditions should be ignored. But the impulse for change will always come from the political sphere, from overcoming ideological underdevelopment and political and social alienation, not from waiting for capitalism to pass by in its economic coffin.

- *To change reality it is crucial to recognize that the fundamental struggle is between the state and 'civil society'.* This is a term that has been little used, but which needs to be developed as part of any contemporary revolutionary analysis. By civil society we mean all the groups and organizations that are not part of the dominant order or the ruling class. Given the fact that the left throughout the Americas (with the exception of Cuba and Nicaragua) has little or no influence over the state, it is imperative to focus on working and organizing in civil society. Democratic revolution requires the mobilization of the bulk of civil society around a common political cause, against the dominant ideology and the traditional political parties that reinforce and sustain the dominant order.

As part of the struggle in civil society we should strive to incorporate all the social forces and all of their demands and needs, including those of the indigenous and ethnic movements, the religious sectors, the youth, students and women. We must deal with their political and cultural interests, as well as their economic demands. We can only do this if we recognize that thought, ideology, and political action are the key elements in any successful revolutionary process.

- *We need to reclaim our revolutionary history*. We have to recuperate what has been creative, especially the collective experiences of the popular sectors in the different revolutionary movements. In forging a new ideology, we ought to scrutinize our history and question everything that may be dogmatic, sectarian and mechanical. We must eliminate our political prejudices.

There is a strong revolutionary tradition throughout the Western Hemisphere, in North America as well as in Latin America and the Caribbean. In the first chapter we will look at the history of twentieth-century revolutionary practice and theory in the Americas to understand the roots of our crisis today. The postulates of Marxism can only come alive if they are used to look at the history of our popular struggles. The pessimism and demoralization that characterize many sectors of the left ought to give way to optimism, based on an understanding of the persistence and depth of the popular struggles in the Americas. It is our ideological and theoretical immaturity combined with inadequate strategic approaches and a failure to understand our own history that have so often been the stumbling blocks in consolidating revolutionary movements.

Some of the criticisms made by non-Marxists of socialism are valid and need to be taken into account. These should be discussed along with some of the recent criticisms made by socialist leaders like Fidel Castro and Mikhail Gorbachev.

- *Marxism needs revitalization.* In scrutinizing everything, we should not abandon Marxism as a method, nor should we abandon the historic project of revolution and international socialism anchored in the Marxist tradition. The political revisionists in the United States and Latin America who believe we must start anew by discarding most of Marxism do not advance either political realism or the cause of social change. Rather they reinforce existing political fragmentation and abandon historical vision.

Our goal is not merely to be critical of the past but to build from the successes as well as the failures of previous revolutionary movements. A major error of the left political parties as well as intellectuals is that of being hyper-critical. We have criticized our own movements to the point of destructiveness and sectarianism. It is not productive simply to denounce others for not holding the 'correct' position. Our purpose here is to critique the past with the aim of learning from it and developing a new political apppoach.

- *We need to advance internationalism and new revolutionary values.* Today, US imperialism, through the employment of its cultural, economic and political power, has linked the United States, Latin America and the Caribbean into a single totality. This makes it imperative for revolutionaries in these regions to perceive and carry out the revolutionary processes from common perspectives. Just as the right has constructed an ideological conception of the world based on its practice in the past (its failures as well as its successes), so also the left must develop a new vision based on its collective memory and on the struggles of the peoples throughout the Americas.

To mobilize these forces along with the working class we need to incorporate values like liberty, equality, individual creativity, love and solidarity as well as democracy and patriotism. These values should be given new meaning and depth. Because of their idealistic and moral content they have often been neglected or used only rhetorically by revolutionaries. The advance of revolutionary practice has to be accompanied by a strengthening of our ideology and this in turn requires the forging of a new revolutionary morality.

- *Debate is part of the ideological insurrection against capitalism and imperialism.* In this work we do not mean to imply that we have discovered immutable political principles or the 'correct' path' for political struggle. Rather it is our hope that we can help open up a rich political debate, a debate that is badly needed in this period when the New Right is ascendant ideologically. We want this debate to help draw the peoples of the Americas closer together as they confront their common enemies – US imperialism and the local ruling classes.[5]

In the last chapter we discuss the advance of the political revolution today, looking at how it is a revolution with many fronts. It is an insurrection against the dominant culture and ideas, and it is also a continuing protest against economic, social and political structures sustained by repression and indoctrination. This work is itself part of the effort to advance the ideological insurrection that is so vitally needed to challenge capitalism and imperialism as the twentieth century draws to a close.

1

Revolutionary Practice and Theory in the Americas

To bring the democratic vision to life in contemporary revolutionary movements we need to understand the historic legacy of Marxism in the Americas. With the notable exception of Chile, no capitalist country in the hemisphere has a Marxist tradition that is as well rooted as France, Spain or Greece where millions of workers and the major social movements are influenced to one degree or another by Marxism.

The unfortunate reality is that Marxism has not been able to sink deep roots in the Americas. This is not due to any inherent 'unreceptiveness' of the countries of the Western Hemisphere to Marxism (as many US political scientists would have us believe), nor is it due to a lack of serious political organizing by Marxists. We believe that throughout most of this century Marxism has had a limited impact in the Americas because it has not been able to develop a theoretical or strategic approach that responds to the specific conditions that exist in the Americas.

In part this is due to Marxism's European origins. Marx, Engles, Kautsky, Lenin, Luxembourg, Trotsky, Gramsci were all products of an interrelated European history and culture which remained the ground of their revolutionary theory and practice. Until the Cuban Revolution, the Americas had few revolutionary theorists or strategists who attempted to formulate indigenous programs of political struggle. A brief look at the history of the socialist and communist movements in the United States, Latin America and the Caribbean will show just how the Marxist political parties have remained 'underdeveloped' in this respect.

1900–1935: The Rise of Marxism in the Americas

During the early decades of this century movements of the working class and the peasantry in Latin America were influenced primarily by non-Marxist revolutionary traditions. Anarcho-syndicalism, a political philosophy that came to the Americas from Southern Europe (principally from Spain and Italy), was especially influential among the new immigrant proletariat in the Southern Cone countries: Chile, Uruguay and Argentina. In the period around the turn of the twentieth century, general strikes and spirited worker rebellions in these countries were spearheaded by anarcho-syndicalist unions that openly espoused the overthrow of the capitalist system and the smashing of the state.

Radical peasant movements constituted an indigenous form of revolutionary action in the early decades of this century. In southern Mexico Emiliano Zapata led the first modern peasant upheaval. The peasants' demand for land and the breakup of haciendas and plantations constituted an explosive challenge to agrarian capitalism. Although Zapata's movement was defeated, peasant upheavals and cries for land reform continued to echo throughout Latin America. The movements of Peralte in Haiti and Sandino in Nicaragua were other early examples of non-Marxist revolutionary struggles that drew heavily on the peasantry and the rural working class. Both went well beyond demands for land reform in their revolutionary programs, calling for fundamental changes in their governments and for an end to US intervention.

These early revolutionary movements had a profound impact on the development of Marxism. Many of the demands and programs that Marxist revolutionaries espouse today draw on this earlier tradition. The general strike, armed struggle, the use of trade unions as a vehicle for revolutionary activity, the demands for land and decent working conditions, anti-interventionism and anti-imperialism – these were all demands and strategies adopted by the early anarcho-syndicalist, peasant, and non-Marxist revolutionary movements. They constitute the broader revolutionary legacy that influences political movements up to this very day.

Although Latin American socialist parties in the mould of Kautsky and the Second International also appeared in the early twentieth century – especially in the most advanced urban milieux of Chile, Brazil, Argentina and Uruguay – the most interesting example of an early Marxist party was Eugene Debs' Socialist Party of America. Founded in 1901, it was shaped by the bitter union struggles of the US working class, as well as by a long tradition of radical agrarian revolt. The party's proletarian base in the immigrant working class combined with its strong appeal to sectors of poor farmers (especially in Oklahoma) and to the newly emerging middle class made it a potent force in US politics. Socialist trade unionists, representing a third of the unions in the American Federation of Labor, repeatedly challenged the pro-business orientation of Samuel Gompers. In 1912 the Socialist Party reached its high water mark at the polls when it succeeded in electing candidates to over 1200 offices while Debs garnered almost a million votes for president.

The First World War, followed by the Bolshevik revolution in 1917, precipitated upheavals in the Socialist parties everywhere. Already suffering from internal fissures over whether or not to support the war, the Socialists split into two camps over the October Revolution. In the United States, the pro-Bolshevik faction left the Socialist Party in 1919 and set up the Communist Labor Party; and the Communist Party of America, ancestors of the present day Communist Party of the United States of America (CPUSA). Throughout the Americas national sections of the Communist International were formed in the 1920s and the early 1930s. As a group, only the Caribbean isles under colonial domination failed to form Communist parties during this period.

In most cases the new parties had a strong working-class base. In the United States trade-union leaders close to the Communists set up the Trade Union Education League (TUEL) in 1920, a broad alliance of 'class struggle' militants and industrial unionists. The Chilean Communist Party actually emerged out of the Federation of Chilean Workers, the country's largest union federation. And in Brazil, Uruguay, Argentina and other countries trade-union leaders were active in the Communist parties from the very beginning.

During this early period many Communists were in the forefront of the political struggles in their countries, particularly in the late 1920s and early 1930s when the Great Depression created a mass of unemployed and immiserated workers throughout the Americas. In Chile, the Communist Party found strong support among the miners as well as the urban workers. By the early 1930s it was a major political force in the country, providing leadership in the 1931 general strike that toppled the dictatorship of Carlos Ibanez and ushered in a new era in Chilean politics.

In Central America and the Caribbean, Communists concentrated on organizing the plantation workers, particularly in the banana enclaves run by US multinationals. In the 1920s and 1930s, tens of thousands of workers rose up in rebellion against the exploitative working and living conditions imposed by these multinationals. The subsequent repression of the trade unions and the Communist parties, usually by the local military forces under the direction of the corporations, resulted in the deaths of thousands of workers. In some cases the unions and the Communist parties were destroyed. But they left vital legacies and to this day the local Communist parties are active in many of the plantation trade unions.

The young Salvadoran Communist Party under the leadership of Sandino's former comrade-in-arms, Farabundo Marti, in 1932 led a massive uprising by workers and campesinos against the country's brutal oligarchic regime. The boldness of the insurgents, who demanded a new political system in which the peasants and the workers would be ascendant, led the Salvadoran oligarchy to demand the bloody repression of the rebellion. The reins of government were turned over to General Martinez who launched the infamous 'matanza', slaughtering over 20,000 people.

In the United States, the Communist party figured prominently in the social struggles of the early 1930s. The first nationwide protest against unemployment was organized by the Communist party in 1930, with an estimated 1.25 million workers participating in rallies and demonstrations across the country. The militant strikes of farmworkers in California and sharecroppers in Alabama, the longshoremen's Pacific coast strike that culminated in the general strike in San Francisco in 1934 and the historic GM sitdown strike of 1937 – these and many other labor struggles were led by Communists, playing a central role in the forging of industrial unionism.

Mariátegui's Challenge

The struggles of the 1920s opened a political debate that continues today. At issue is the very content of socialism and the strategy and tactics that should be used to achieve it. This debate was broadly outlined by two Peruvians, José Carlos Mariátegui and Victor Raúl Haya de la Torre. Each of them advocated profound, radical change and each believed that the oligarchy and imperialism were the peoples' implacable foes. The differences between their revolutionary programs lay principally in the nature of the class alliances they advocated. These differences were played out in the political parties that each founded: Mariátegui helped establish Peru's first Communist Party while Haya de la Torre set up APRA, the Popular Alliance for Revolution in the Americas.

Mariátegui's Marxism involved a highly original attempt to respond to the specific political conditions existing in Peru and South America. In the mid-1920s, during the dictatorship of Leguía, he established the periodical *Amauta* which became famous all over Latin America as a forum for radical debate. Mariátegui was especially concerned with the role of the Indians, who comprised over half of Peru's population. In his major work, *Seven Interpretative Essays on Peruvian Reality* (1928), he argued that the Indian peasantry could not simply be subordinated to the workers in any revolutionary struggle, and that the key to successful political work in the countryside lay in understanding the cultural and social values sustained by the Indian communities.[1]

In the 1920s Mariátegui and Haya de la Torre became enmeshed in a political debate that focused on the issue of class alliances and the role of the working class in revolutionary struggle. Haya de la Torre, while recognizing the need to organize workers, argued that the middle classes had to be incorporated in any political process. He rejected the centrality of class struggle and asserted that virtually all classes should unite in a broad front to oppose the oligarchy and their principal imperialist allies, the multinational corporations. Mariátegui on the other hand saw the worker–Indian alliance as the axis on which any challenge to the existent order had to be built. While recognizing that the struggles against the oligarchy and imperialism were crucial, he maintained that these conflicts alone should not determine class alliances, and accused APRA of becoming the 'Kuomintang of Latin America'.

APRA, which was founded in 1930, was very militant in its early years. But Haya de la Torre's refusal to acknowledge the role of class struggle soon led it down the reformist and accomodationist path. It abandoned its belief that the multinationals were a threat to the country, and it came to focus on the Peruvian military as the main antagonist, particularly after it blocked APRA's rise to power in the 1930s.

Although Mariátegui's writings and example influenced succeeding generations of Marxists in Peru and Latin America, their immediate political impact on the Communist movement was limited. In 1928 Mariátegui and a group of intellectuals and trade unionists had founded the Socialist Party of Peru, which affiliated to the Third International. However, in 1929 Mariátegui came into conflict with the Comintern over his theses and the type of party structure that was most appropriate for Peru. Before the dispute was decided, Mariátegui died and the party split, with the majority deciding to follow the Comintern line as the Communist Party of Peru.

The Decline of the Communist Movement

While the trajectory of APRA demonstrated that a party that did not support class struggle and a proletarian project would lose its revolutionary claims, the Communist parties in the 1920s and 1930s found it difficult to devise a strategy for building a broad system of class alliances that did not betray the objective of a socialist revolution. The Communist parties were often torn by the inherent tensions in two conflicting political tendencies: when the parties maintained a strict political commitment to the working class and a proletarian project, they usually failed to capture the support of other social sectors. But when they moved to expand their alliances, they often found themselves indefinitely postponing a socialist program and subordinating themselves to a bourgeois-reformist program.

These two tendencies played themselves out in the 1930s. By the early years of that decade the Communist parties of the Western Hemisphere had built strong bases of support among sections of the working class by pursuing a program that made few concessions to other social sectors. The parties were noted for their high degree of militancy in challenging the capitalist order, but they were unable to forge the broad political alliances that could take them to power on a socialist platform.

This political approach shifted in the Popular Front years, a period that started in the mid-1930s when the Third International, or the Comintern, urged all its member parties to enter into political coalitions with bourgeois parties to confront Fascism. The Popular Front strategy may have made sense in Europe where Fascism was intent upon liquidating its opponents, particularly the Communist parties, the trade unions, and ultimately the only socialist country, the Soviet Union. But in some countries in the Americas, the Communist parties wound up sacrificing their militant programs for political alliances that were of questionable value in advancing the class struggle.

In the case of Chile, Comintern representatives compelled the Chilean Communist party to adopt a Popular Front strategy that in 1938 included entrance into a political coalition that supported the presidential candidacy of Pedro Aguirre Cerda, a wealthy landowner from the right wing of the moderate, Radical party. The coalition won the election, and the Communist party assumed cabinet positions in the new government. But its militant historic trajectory was compromised; the party became less combative at the base and began to be seduced by sharing political power in the bourgeois political system.

In the United States, the Popular Front strategy had initially almost the reverse effect. The decision to work with all progressive political organizations enabled the CPUSA to broaden its mass work and become a key force in building the new militant labor confederation, the Congress of Industrial Organizations (CIO). Party members held no important positions in the Roosevelt administration and accordingly they were not deluded by the possibility of sharing power with a reformist government. The party instead focused on anti-fascist mass work and on winning over new members. This was the era when the party organized the Abraham

Lincoln Brigade, the US volunteers who went to fight side by side with the Republican army against the Fascists in Spain.

But much of this work was shattered by the Comintern's decision to abandon the anti-fascist strategy in 1939 when the Soviet Union signed a surprise non-aggression pact with Nazi Germany. Here again, the strategy may have made sense for the Soviet Union which needed time to build up its defenses against a German invasion, but it had adverse effects on Communist parties in other parts of the world. In the United States, it undermined years of work by the CPUSA and alienated thousands of sympathizers who had been attracted by its anti-fascist organizing. The full consequences of this zig-zag policy were felt a decade later when the US ruling class launched the Cold War and painted the Communist Party as anti-American because of its ties to the Soviet Union.

The submission of the Communist parties in the Americas to the policies of the Comintern reflected a fundamental weakness of Marxism in the Americas – its inability to develop and sustain an indigenous revolutionary strategy. While broad class alliances were certainly necessary at different stages in the 1930s and 1940s, they should have been determined by the needs of the struggle at the local or national level, rather than being dictated for all by the Comintern.

The problem was that during the very years when the Communist movement reached its apogee in this hemisphere – the 1920s and 1930s – it failed to produce its own body of Marxist theoreticians capable of developing political programs and strategies suited to the specific political conditions faced by Communists in their respective countries. There were organic intellectuals in the parties who made invaluable contributions, such as Mariátegui in Peru and Julio Antonio Mella in Cuba, but in large part the intellectual work that emerged in the Americas was a mere adaptation of political ideas and strategies developed in Europe.

Nationalism, Populism and Reformism

The development of APRA was symptomatic of the national-populist movements and leaderships that emerged in the 1930s, 1940s and 1950s to channel the mass movements in reformist directions. Without revolutionary parties capable of providing indigenous revolutionary alternatives, the masses throughout the Americas turned increasingly to charismatic populist leaders like Getulio Vargas in Brazil in the 1930s and 1940s, and Juan Domingo Peron in Argentina in the 1940s and 1950s. In the United States, the forging of a new Democratic Party coalition in the 1930s and 1940s with a strong working class base also illustrated the tendency of mass movements to be subordinated in reformist coalitions.

But as was noted earlier, there were radical non-Communist leaders in the inter-war period who remained committed to profound political and social changes. Of these Augusto César Sandino was the most outstanding. For seven years he led his rural insurgents against the US Marines who had invaded Nicaragua in the era of Coolidge and Hoover's 'Dollar Diplomacy'. Mobilizing workers as well as peasants under his anti-imperialist banner, Sandino planted the seeds of revolutionary nationalism and he nurtured the rise of militant solidarity movements in Latin America and even in the United States. Like Zapata earlier, he and most of the leadership of his rebel army were treacherously murdered (by Somoza) while negotiating with the government.

Another major non-Communist radical whose influence survives today was Jorge Eliecer Gaitan of Colombia. In the 1940s he demanded profound social changes that would benefit the masses. In 1948 he too was murdered, setting off *la Violencia*: the civil war and political upheaval that still rocks Colombia today.

Unhappily, the Communist parties largely did not tap this strain of radical populist militancy in the Americas. Indeed, by the 1940s and 1950s the Communists, in an effort to compete with the bourgeois reformist parties, had abandoned most of their revolutionary program and were adapting to reformist political illusions. This tendency was tragically illustrated by political developments in Guatemala in 1950 to 1954. When Jacobo Arbenz was elected president of Guatemala in 1950, the Workers' Party of Guatemala (the official name of the country's Communist party) put forth the thesis that Guatemala was still in the feudal stage of development. Thus, before a socialist revolution could be carried out, capitalism had to implant itself. In Guatemala this meant that the party embraced the government and program of Jacobo Arbenz which sought to develop the country along capitalist lines by nourishing the growth of the petty bourgeoisie and capitalist industry. The agrarian reform law, which called for the expropriation and redistribution of idle and untilled lands, was part of this development program. The Communist party was politically astute enough to realize that this and other reforms of the Arbenz government should be supported, but it was unable to assume leadership of the process or to prevent the tragic disaster that ensued.

The Guatemalan Communist party's enthusiasm for Arbenz's reformist program blinded it to the profound threat posed by US imperialism at the height of the first Cold War. Certainly United Fruit exercised a huge influence on US policy towards Arbenz. But Washington, in any case, was determined not to allow Communists in a Latin American government, even if they were supportive of capitalist development. When the CIA launched its coup against the Arbenz government in June 1954, the Workers' party was caught off guard. There was virtually no resistance and a new government was installed by the United States that brutally outlawed the Workers' Party and the popular organizations affiliated with it, unleasing a cycle of repression that continues today.

In the 1940s and 1950s the established Communist parties, whether in the United States, Argentina, Mexico or Peru made virtually no innovations in revolutionary theory. The same was true of many of the other communist formations that had emerged, of which the most significant were the Trotskyist parties. Like the original Communist parties linked to the Comintern, these splinter formations continued to define their political line around international issues, especially their position vis-a-vis the Soviet Union. While often defending a more democratic interpretation of Leninism, they had little to offer in terms of original revolutionary theory and practice on the terrains of their own societies.

In this same period, the nationalist revolution in Bolivia demonstrated the limits and pitfalls of movements that are led by radicalized sectors of the petty bourgeoisie when they are not developed ideologically or organically linked to a socialist project. The Revolution of 1952, led by the National Revolutionary Movement (MNR), incorporated the miners, the peasants, and nationalist, anti-imperialist sectors of the petty bourgeoisie. But the MNR's program was ultimately reformist, dominated by petty bourgeois interests. It effectively bridled the more radical elements and failed to challenge US imperialism or to alter the fundamental conditions of poverty and exploitation that existed in the country.

The Failure of Progressive Movements in the US

In the United States the nadir of the Communist movement came in the 1950s. The wave of economic prosperity for the white population in the late 1940s and in the 1950s, combined with the McCarthy witch-hunts, were key factors in the development of an atmosphere of social conformism that had little or no tolerance for radical political movements. Critical mistakes had been made by Communist and other progressive social forces in the United States that facilitated the indoctrination of a deep-seated anti-communism in broad segments of the US populace. The fatal decision of the CPUSA to support the Stalin-Hitler pact in 1938 was compounded by its support for the 'no-strike' pledge during World War II and by its uncritical endorsement of Stalin's policies after the war. This fed into the hands of the crusade of anti-communists to brand the CPUSA as representing Soviet rather than American national interests.

Other radical forces in the United States were also adversely affected by difficult decisions made prior to the Second World War.

The pacifist and anti-war sectors had enjoyed considerable influence among the American people in the 1930s because most of the populace felt that the First World War had not really been a war 'to make the world safe for democracy'. Many recognized that US participation in the 'Great War' had only played into European power rivalries and had filled the coffers of the munitions manufacturers. But in the 1930s these pacifist and anti-war forces failed to understand that the world was changing, that Hitler and Fascism were insidious political forces that had to be confronted militarily. In the aftermath of the Second World War the pacifists who opposed the use of military force abroad were easily discredited. Accused of being 'isolationists' and of 'appeasing totalitarian movements', the pacifists and other anti-war forces were unable to build a strong political or social base to resist the growth of the US military industrial complex and the national security state.

The Revolutionary Wave of the 1960s

Given the crisis of the Communist parties in the Western Hemisphere, it was almost inevitable that a new revolutionary dynamism would come from political movements that had little or nothing to do with traditional Marxism. The triumph of the Cuban Revolution opened a new era in revolutionary struggle. Employing the strategy of guerrilla warfare, the 26th of July Movement seized power on a broad anti-dictatorial program. While the new Cuban leadership did not use the traditional theoretical framework of Marxism Leninism to guide its early actions, it did recognize two salient points that are central for any revolutionary struggle in the Americas: 1) the necessity of tapping the long tradition of democratic, popular and anti-imperialist sentiments that had shaped the popular consciousness for years throughout the hemisphere, and 2) the need to combine armed struggle with the development of mass movements.

Washington's opposition to these principles and to the new government's economic and social reforms quickly radicalized the revolution and compelled it to look to the Soviet Union for support. The Cuban leadership had learned well the central lesson of the Guatemalan experience from 1950 to 1954: that a revolution could survive only if it was willing to mobilize its total human and material resources to confront US imperialism.

The Castro-Guevarist approach marked an important advance in the theory and practice of revolution. It emphasized the strategic importance of the peasantry, of armed struggle, and of an alliance with students in the cities. Guevarism broke decisively with the reductionistic approach of the Communist parties, which argued that a socialist revolution was not possible until capitalism had fully developed the forces of production and had created a modern working class. The new revolutionaries correctly argued that economic backwardness in Latin America in fact facilitated a revolutionary process rather that serving as an obstacle. Another major contribution of Guevarism and the Cuban revolution was to reveal the potentiality (and the necessity) of linking a political revolution in one country to revolutionary movements throughout the Americas. The Cuban experience also demonstrated that strong relations with the socialist bloc countries were essential if a revolutionary movement was to survive against imperialism.²

Due in large part to the success of the Cuban revolution, the decade of the 1960s was a period of rich political and intellectual ferment in Latin America and the Caribbean. The Cuban Revolution demonstrated for the first time in the Americas that a socialist political revolution could take place in a small underdeveloped country on the doorstep of the United States. This inspired other revolutionaries to take up arms, particularly in Guatemala, Nicaragua, Venezuela, Colombia and Bolivia.

The United States, of course, did not stand idly by in the face of this historic threat. It launched the Alliance for Progress in an effort to reform some of the antiquated structures of Latin America, and it undertook a counter-insurgency program to eradicate the rural guerrilla movements. The most notable success of this program occurred in Bolivia in 1967 when Che Guevara was captured and killed. Two years earlier, the Johnson administration had shown the limits of permissible reform when it invaded the Dominican Republic and suppressed the urban insurrection led by Col. Camano and a faction of the Dominican army.

1967–1977: The Revolution Moves South and Into the Cities

After the defeat of the rural based guerrilla movements in the mid and late 1960s, the revolutionary and social movements began to gather force in the cities, particularly in South America, where urban capitalism was much more advanced than in the Caribbean Basin. There, the multinational corporations and the national bourgeoisies had already created a large industrial proletariat.

Efforts were made to adopt *foquismo* to these urban realities, particularly by Carlos Marighella, who wrote the *Mini-Manual of the Urban Guerrilla* in early 1969. Although Marighella was soon killed in combat, the Tupamaros in Uruguay succeeded in creating a complex urban guerrilla infrastructure, and through a series of spectacular actions captured the imagination of the world. However even the Tupamaros proved incapable of dealing with the systematic, mass repression unleashed through the application of US counterinsurgency warfare. By the time of the Uruguayan military coup in 1972, the ranks of the Tupamaros had been decimated and the country's military rulers proceeded to eradicate the units that remained. The experience of the Tupamaros and other revolutionary movements demonstrated that the most difficult challenge is that of mounting a revolutionary insurgency in the urban centers. It is there that capitalism is the strongest, and it is there that the revolutionary movements so often meet with defeat – not simply because of the strength of the military, but also because the bourgeoisie exercises a high degree of political control and ideological influence over the cities.

In the early 1970s the efforts to develop new revolutionary projects focused on Chile and Argentina. Although the popular movements in each country led to military coups and massive repression, the experiences in Chile and Argentina provided important lessons for movements throughout the hemisphere.

In Chile the election of Salvador Allende in 1970 marked the first time in the Americas that a government was peacefully elected to power on a socialist platform. In the Allende years two major strategic positions were debated on the Chilean left. The main position, articulated most clearly by the Communist party, but endorsed by most of the parties in the Popular Unity government of Allende, maintained that the transition to socialism required expanded juridical control over the principal holdings of the bourgeoisie and the transnational corporations, and the construction of a popular movement that would support these actions and prevent the military and the bourgeoisie from violating the constitution.

The other position, put forth by the Movement of the Revolutionary Left (MIR), argued that socialism could not be consolidated without armed struggle – eventually there would have to be a violent confrontation with the bourgeoisie and its military allies.[3] By late 1972 the Communist party and the rest of the Popular Unity government, due largely to pressures by militant workers within their own ranks, began to recognize that there would probably be an armed confrontation. But they, like the MIR, believed that it would be possible to split the army with certain sectors coming over to the revolutionary movement. This analysis was invalidated in September 1973 when Augusto Pinochet maintained the unity of the armed forces and overthrew the government of Salvador Allende. The full weight of the new dictatorship now fell squarely on all revolutionary organizations. Within a year much of the MIR leadership had been killed or forced into exile and its popular organizations had been dealt heavy blows.

In Argentina, as in Chile, there were two distinct revolutionary positions over how to take advantage of the openings provided by the Peronist governments of the early 1970s. The Montoneros, the radicalized youth wing of the Peronist party, argued that the struggle for political power had to be waged within the trade unions and the broader Peronist movement. The Popular Revolutionary Army (ERP), on the other hand, while initially a Trotskyist organization that sought to organize within the trade unions, opted in the early 1970s for a strategy of rural guerrilla warfare. Antagonistic towards the Peronist youth movement, the ERP maintained that the Montonero program was reformist and that Peronism and the entire state apparatus would have to be confronted in order to seize state power.

Although the Montoneros and the ERP were able to build large organizations with tens of thousands of members, they were eventually crushed by the Argentine military. The general problem for the revolutionary movements in Argentina, as well as the rest of the Southern Cone, was that the military remained monolithic and willing, with broad support of the bourgeoisie, to engage in Nazi-style repression of the popular left. In none of the countries was the crisis of the state apparatus deep enough to enable the revolutionary movements to seize power through politico-military organizing.

The Resurgence of Revolutionary Movements in the Caribbean Basin

After the revolutionary defeats and the rise of the military regimes in the Southern Cone, the revolutionary pendulum swung back northward, to Central America. During the 1960s and 1970s, under the aegis of the Alliance for Progress and the multinational corporations, a surge of capital expansion occurred in both the cities and the countryside of Central America. The displacement of peasants by agribusiness plantations, combined with import-substitution industrialization in the cities, resulted in a flood of rural migrants to the urban areas. Many, however, found only marginal employment and were forced to exist on the fringes of society.[4]

In three countries – Guatemala, El Salvador and Nicaragua – this social upheaval fueled an upsurge in revolutionary activity. Guerrilla movements regrouped or emerged in the rural areas in these countries in the early 1970s, and by the end of the decade they had moved into the major cities where they had established important bases of support. In the case of Nicaragua, the urban movement and the urban insurrections in 1978 and 1979 were decisive factors in toppling the Somoza regime and bringing the Sandinista Front to power.

Simultaneously in the Caribbean there was an upsurge in nationalist, anti-imperialist movements, often linked to progressive sectors of the armed forces and to sectors of the petit bourgeoisie. Omar Torijos in Panama, Maurice Bishop in Grenada, Bouterse in Guyana, and Manley in Jamaica were all manifestations of the strong anti-imperialist current at work in the Caribbean in the 1970s and 1980s.

Political Revival in the US

Like Latin America, the decade of the 1960s in the United States was a period of rich social and intellectual ferment that renewed radical movements, outside the influence of the orthodox Communist movement. Initially, the principal motors of the revival of radical politics in the United States were the Black civil rights movement and the youth movement. The civil rights struggles of the early 1960s, which demanded an end to voting discrimination and equal access to public facilities, represented the first serious challenge to the US political establishment in the aftermath of the Second World War. As the movement gained momentum, it disrupted the Jim Crow social system in the South and sowed seeds of discontent in the northern cities, where Blacks were subject to rampant housing and job discrimination. The movement demonstrated to the entire world that a major sector of US society – its Black population – had been left out of the 'American dream'. For some in the white community, particularly students in the northern universities who participated in demonstrations and voter registration campaigns, the civil rights movement shook the democratic ideals they had grown up with and revealed that repression, poverty and exploitation were integral aspects of US capitalism.

The Vietnam war resistance, which had an equally dramatic impact on US society, was profoundly influenced by the Black insurgency. Students for a Democratic Society (SDS), which was initially a social democratic-sponsored organization, galvanized American youth during the early days of the civil rights movement to question many aspects of democratic capitalism. In 1962 SDS released the Port Huron statement which called for an end to 'unreasoning anti-communism' and the forging of a 'new left' comprised of socialists and liberals who would build a participatory democracy in the United States. These principles propelled SDS into the leadership of the anti-war movement in 1965 when it organized the first massive march on Washington against the Vietnam war. SDS's insistence that no communist organizations be excluded from participation led to an irrevocable break with the old social democratic and liberal organizations that had helped forge the anti-communist consensus in the United States.

The prolonged agony of the war in Vietnam provided fertile grounds for the revitalization of Marxist thought in the United States. The initial assertion by some liberals that the war was a 'mistake' that could be corrected by electing better leaders began to wear thin as American casualties mounted and the Pentagon escalated its air war to a genocidal fury. Many Americans began to look for deeper causes of the war, and Marxist thought, with its explanation of the imperialist nature of capitalist societies, began to have a wider appeal. The works of radical scholars – like C. Wright Mills, the founder of radical sociology in the United States, William Appleman Williams who put forth a neo-Marxist analysis of US history, and Harry Magdoff, author of *The Age of Imperialism* – helped educate a whole new generation of Americans.[5]

The reawakening of radical thought in the United States took many forms and was in no way dominated by any one political party or particular school of Marxist thought. Indeed, the social and intellectual upheaval of the 1960s precipitated a wide range of political movements and approaches, many of which were eclectic and voluntaristic. SDS itself split into several factions, of which the smallest but most publicized were the Weathermen. Its members attempted to open a domestic front of the Vietnam war by placing bombs at corporate and military sites. Meanwhile the Black Panthers proclaimed the right of Blacks to engage in the 'armed defense' of their communities. A number of new communist organizations and networks also emerged such as the Revolutionary Communist Party (pro-Maoist) and the Trend (led by the Philadelphia Workers Organizing Committee).

Radical thought flourished on the campuses, with many universities possessing one or more underground newspapers publishing a wide array of alternative materials on pop music, sex, politics and the anti-war movement. More serious publications and research organizations also appeared in the 1960s and early 1970s, such as *Radical America*, the Union of Radical Political Economists (URPE), the *Insurgent Sociologist*, the North American Congress on Latin America (NACLA), and the Middle Eastern Research Institute (MERIP); they developed a wide range of Marxist or radical analyses.

Placed in historical perspective, the political upheaval of the 1960s and the early 1970s had two important effects on US society. On the one hand it nurtured the development of an array of Marxist thinkers and theorists, many of whom were able to secure positions in universities or affiliated research centers from which they continued to develop Marxist thought. Simultaneously, the social discontent and political questioning of the 1960s enabled a number of powerful single issue social movements to arise. The emergence of feminism and the women's movement, the rise of new union movements like the United Farm Workers in California, and the development of a Gay rights movement – these movements together with the Black movement, the solidarity organizations and the anti-war movement made a powerful force for change in the United States.

By the end of the 1970s, however, both the new social movements and Marxist thought were thrown on the defensive. A major problem was that no real symbiosis occurred between the different social movements and Marxism. They each operated in different spheres. While the Marxists were based primarily on campuses or directed small publishing and research centers, the social movements concerned themselves with concrete issues and looked increasingly to the liberal wing of the Democratic party to redress their grievances. None of the old or new Marxist-Leninist parties was able to bridge this gap. Some of them made sustained efforts to organize in the workplace and trade unions. But most Marxist parties were more concerned with debating who had the 'correct political line' and which political organization was destined to be the 'vanguard' of the American revolution (preferably with a franchise from Beijing). None of the parties developed strong social bases to become a force in American political life. To this day the central issue remains that of developing a political strategy to mobilize and unify the different single issue movements so that they pose an alternative, mass pole.

The Development of Marxist Theory in the Americas

Precisely because the organized Marxist left failed to develop its own body of native theoreticians in the earlier part of this century, it was from the universities and small groups of independent Marxian theorists that the most creative Marxist thinking began to emerge in the 1950s. In the Americas the *Monthly Review* school was in the forefront of this process and played a critical role in preserving Marxist thought at a historic moment when it was under siege.

Paul Sweezy, a founder of *Monthly Review* in 1949, had earlier authored *The Theory of Capitalist Development*, a comprehensive Marxist overview of how the capitalist system functioned. It adapted Marxist theory to twentieth century economic realities, and for years it was the principal text in the United States for those who wanted to understand Marxism.[6] Subsequently Paul Baran, another founder of *Monthly Review*, took up the issue of the impact of imperialism on underdeveloped countries. He argued that monopoly capital would hold back the forces of innovation and production in the underdeveloped countries. The fact that the monopolies had developed large economies of scale had dire consequences for the third world countries; only a few industries (foreign or locally owned) would be needed to supply the relatively small local markets. Under these conditions, the competitive forces of capitalism would be held back, which meant that capitalism would develop much more slowly in the third world than it had in nineteenth century Europe.[7] This theoretical approach led to a breakthrough in the next decade when a new wave of political ferment would hit the United States, Latin America and the Caribbean.

Marxist theory took a major leap forward in the 1960s with the advent of the dependency school. This theoretical framework was in many ways the counterpart of the *foco* theory in its analysis of the political economy of imperialism and the third world. Like the *foquistas*, the dependency theorists broke with many of the dogmas of the Communist parties. The *dependistas*, as they were called, denied that a country had to go through a stage of dynamic capitalist development before socialist revolution could occur. They argued that Latin America was already integrated into the world market and that intensive capitalist exploitation had already been occurring for centuries. Only a socialist revolution that expropriated the transnational corporations and the local ruling classes could break these ties and lead the third world societies along the path of autonomous and sustained development.

In retrospect, dependency theory was especially important because it marked the first fundamentally new school of thought on political economy to be developed with contributions from radical intellectuals in both the United States and Latin America. First Paul Baran and *Monthly Review* laid the key building block for dependency theory in *The Political Economy of Growth*, arguing that true capitalist development was blocked in much of the third world by the predominance of multinational capital. Subsequently, Andre Gunder Frank carried these premises one step further and argued that the historic domination of Latin America by foreign capital meant the continual 'development of underdevelopment': i.e. the metropolitan centers would always drain resources out of the peripheral countries, thereby keeping them in a perpetual state of underdevelopment.[8] Latin Americans like Teotonio Dos Santos and Rui Mauro Marini then began to use dependency theory to show how dependency shaped the internal social and political formations of third world societies.[9] By the early 1970s virtually every major university in the United States and in Latin America was influenced in some way by dependency theory, and virtually all revolutionary parties or organizations, including the Communist parties, had adopted dependency theory as their framework for understanding the relations between the metropolitan centers and the periphery.

However, by the mid-1970s dependency theory was being challenged. Marxists linked to the publication *Latin American Perspectives*, along with political economists from Mexico, Peru and other countries in Latin America, argued that the tremendous differences in social and productive structures that existed in each country could not be accounted for simply by the spheres of trade and commerce as the *dependistas* had done. Robert Brenner also made a decisive contribution to this debate by looking at how trade had historically exerted only a limited influence on the rise of capitalism, which he attributed to the more central dynamic of agrarian class struggle. Social formations varied from country to country, not because of different patterns of international trade, but because of the differences in the internal development of the forces of production.

The Lessons of the Past

The rich inter-American debate over dependency theory focused on issues relating to the political economy of capitalism while contributing very little to the understanding of concrete political processes. Marxism, while it has now firmly implanted itself in the intellectual tradition of the Americas, is still not an integral part of the broader political discourse. And since the upheaval of the 1960s and the emergence of the *foco* theory, there have been no major breakthroughs in political theory. There have been important political experiences, including the insurrection in Nicaragua, and the current struggle in El Salvador, but we have barely begun to reflect on and understand what these experiences teach us. Many revolutionaries have learned from the political mistakes of the 1970s; the case of Chile was particularly illustrative in showing how the electoral road to socialism failed. But these are negative lessons, lessons that do not necessarily point to specific strategies for the future.

However, by looking at the broad sweep of revolutionary struggle in the Americas throughout this century, we can gain some insights that may help us. One clear lesson is that each generation has to reassess and rethink the political strategies that are handed down to it. We can learn from the past, but we shouldn't become its prisoners. The role of the Communist parties in the Americas vividly illustrates this. By the beginning of the Second World War these parties had lost their capacity to serve as a motor of revolution in the Americas. They moved in reformist directions and were no longer at the heart of revolutionary struggle as they had often been in the 1920s and 1930s.

It is particularly noteworthy that the two revolutionary movements that actually seized power in the Americas – the 26th of July Movement in Cuba and the Sandinista Front in Nicaragua — were neither self-proclaimed Marxist-Leninist parties when they took power nor in fact did many of their leaders consider themselves Marxist-Leninists. These revolutions drew on the radical political traditions of their own countries to come up with successful strategies for seizing power.

A serious problem for revolutionaries today stems from the fact that since the early part of this century Marxism-Leninism has been identified with the evolution of post-revolutionary society in the Soviet Union. The party and state structures that were implanted in the Soviet Union were generally viewed as the model for other revolutionary societies to follow. Given the problems that developed in the Soviet Union – Stalin's domination, and purges of the Soviet Communist party, the program of forced industrialization, the liquidation of the Kulak class – the close identity of Marxism-Leninism with the Soviet experience soon created tremendous ideological and political problems for revolutionary movements elsewhere. To this day the leaders of the capitalist countries use the Soviet experience to discredit Marxist revolutionary movements.

A related problem stems from the fact that most Marxist-Leninists have defined themselves by their international perspectives rather than by the concrete issues of their own societies. The Third International considered itself to be the ultimate authority on just how Marxism-Leninism should be applied in all revolutionary struggles around the world. But when differences and splits emerged, such as the split between Trotsky and Stalin in the late 1920s, each new revolutionary formation proclaimed that its interpretation of Marxism-Leninism was the correct one. Instead of engaging in a concrete analysis of political, economic and social conditions in each country, many parties and theorists were caught up in the debate over who was really following the 'correct political line'. The debates over Trotskyism, Maoism, Titoism, and even *foquismo* often divided the revolutionary parties over international issues with each camp proclaiming that it alone was the real guardian of revolutionary thought and practice.

Another important historical lesson is that theory can distort revolutionary practice rather than guide it. This was the case with *foquismo*. By focusing on the Cuban revolution and the initial endeavors of the handful of men who led it, the *foquistas* misled many revolutionaries in the Americas into believing that they too could carry out a revolution with a small but determined group of people. This perspective was reinforced by the obsession of many political activists in the early 1970s, particularly in the United States, with the role played by Lenin in the Bolshevik revolution. They saw him as a solitary figure who, through his iron will and clear vision, was able to persevere and lead the Bolshevik party to power. Regardless of whether or not this view of Lenin is correct, it led many revolutionaries to believe that they could adopt a political strategy and resolutely carry it to completion, no matter what the political realities.

This leads to a broader problem: once a revolutionary political theory has been developed it often tends to limit the imagination of future leaders rather than to guide them. This is not to deny the importance of theory. But it does mean that we have to be constantly on guard to ensure that theory does not become dogma. Each new revolutionary struggle and movement must rethink its premises and its theoretical approach as well as its practice. This is only possible if we apply the Marxist method in the most creative manner, without relying on dogma or letting preconceptions distort our understanding.

Che Guevara recognized the role and limits of theory in the Cuban Revolution when he wrote:

> ... this revolution is different. In the minds of some it is an exception to one of the fundamental tenets of orthodox theory. That tenet, as enunciated by Lenin, holds that without revolutionary theory there can be no revolution. We must recognize, however, that revolutionary theory, in as much as it reflects conditions in a society, transcends any statement of that theory. In other words, a revolution can proceed based on accurate historical

analysis and skillful balancing of the forces involved without its theoretical framework ever having been enunciated. To be sure, an adequate statement of theory does simplify the process and helps avoid dangerous pitfalls, provided that statement is in fact correct.[10]

2

Socialism and the Democratic Banner

Today democracy is at the center of the ideological battle between capitalism and socialism. Historically, the United States and its local ruling allies have usually responded to economic and political crises by imposing civilian or military dictators. This was true in the 1930s during the Great Depression, and it was also true during the decade and a half after the Cuban Revolution, when over three-quarters of the inhabitants of Latin America and the Caribbean fell under dictatorial rule as the United States and its local allies sought to repress the mass movements and the guerrilla insurgencies. But in the late 1970s this strategy shifted as the Nicaraguan revolutionaries seized power and the popular classes became increasingly assertive throughout the Americas. Instead of imposing or sustaining dictators as an automatic response to the ever deepening crises, the United States stood by and watched several of them fall. The withdrawal of the military in Argentina, Brazil, Uruguay and Peru, and the downfall of Duvalier in Haiti all attest to this shift in strategy.

To back such dictatorial regimes now means to lose credibility and legitimacy with the masses and to set the scene for the potential collapse of the bourgeois state itself. Thus in the Philippines, another region which the United States has dominated, the Reagan administration abandoned Marcos and is today trying to consolidate the Aquino government around a pro-US platform. The United States is in part compelled to champion 'democracy' because it can offer few economic palliatives. Due to the ever deepening fiscal crisis in the United States, the days of the Alliance for Progress – when the United States could send billions in economic aid to prop up pro-US regimes – are long gone. Also gone are the times when US multinationals and banks rushed to Latin America and the Caribbean with tens of billions of dollars in new investments and loans. Today the United States can offer little economic assistance, only austerity programs and limited bail outs for a few US-proxy governments like Honduras, Jamaica, El Salvador and Costa Rica.[1]

In this political and ideological battle a major tactic of the United States is the sponsoring of controlled democratic elections and the restructuring of governments to give them a reformist facade. Central America is the showcase for this project: there the United States is directly financing elections, bankrolling its favorite politicians (usually through the CIA), and placing US advisers in key government ministries in an effort to modernize the state bureaucracies.

As Contragate has richly revealed, an integral part of this democractic game is the attempt to penetrate and control the institutions of civil society, be they trade unions, political parties, the press corps, the churches, or professional and academic institutions. US public relations experts and psychological operations (psychops) specialists are brought in to work with local governments in an effort to manipulate the media and to control public opinion. Over the international air waves, the United States uses the Voice of America, Radio Marti (beamed at the Caribbean), and even local radio stations (also funded by the CIA) to broadcast its pro-US and anti-communist messages to the local populace. (This is actually the program laid out by the Kissinger Commission in its 1984 report on the situation in Central America. US media coverage of the Kissinger Report focused on the internal Commission debate over aid for the contras. Little attention was paid to the core of the Report which called for the modernization of the Central American states and the creation of societies permeated by American values. This Report is actually one of the more important milestones of Kissinger's career as a defender of the empire. In it he managed to fuse the old liberal program of nation-building in the third world with the ardent anti-communist crusade of the conservatives.)[2]

The left must meet this democratic challenge head on if it is to win the larger war against imperialism. Denouncing dictatorial governments and mounting guerrilla movements against them will no longer be sufficient. There will be few easy targets like Batista, Somoza, or Duvalier. In many parts of the third world the struggle will be fought over democracy, over whether the United States and its reformist allies – be they Duarte in El Salvador or Aquino in the Philippines — can contain the democratic aspirations of the masses and prevent revolutionary alternatives from developing. And the left, to meet this new challenge, will have to take up the democratic banner in a way that it has never done before.

The Quest for the Democratic Banner

US imperialism is in a weak position in the struggle for the democratic banner. The unstable conditions that many of the formal democracies face in Latin America as the economic crisis deepens, the US history of supporting dictators, and the US obsession with preventing any government from coming to power that is open to alliances with the left or with communist political parties – these are factors that make it difficult for the United States to take up the democratic banner without appearing opportunistic and hypocritical. But the left also has a checkered past when it comes to upholding democracy. In both the United States and Latin America the left pays lip service to democracy while rarely developing a concrete program that furthers its advance. Bourgeois domination of the established democratic institutions in the capitalist countries is of course a central reason why the left has largely opted out of the discussion of democracy, particularly when it involves working with existing institutions. But democracy is a potentially revolutionary demand and it is imperative to place it at the head of the revolutionary agenda.

Of course, a major problem for the left is that many 'socialist' governments – in Eastern Europe and the third world – have hardly been ideal democracies. A limited degree of participatory democracy may exist at the base level, but most Communist parties tend to be authoritarian and have even become self-perpetuating elites. The only way for the bulk of the population to influence policy is by making their interests known at the factory or in the community organizations.

In non-revolutionary societies, like those of Latin America, left parties proclaim their commitment to the popular sectors and democracry, but they have sometimes focused more on mounting guerrilla attacks on government institutions than on working in the mass movements. *Foquismo*, the belief that a small band of guerrillas could topple a government, was the most extreme manifestation of this militaristic tendency in the 1960s and 1970s. Even today some politico-military organizations in Latin America display a preoccupation with military operations and deemphasize the importance of mass work.

Other left parties, while not caught up in the idealization of guerrilla warfare, are more concerned with sectarian disputes than they are with developing a democratic program reflecting the concrete interests and needs of the masses. The left in Mexico has sometimes reflected this tendency. The Mexican government and the ruling party, the Institutional Revolutionary Party (PRI), are in the midst of a profound crisis of legitimacy. But the left is fractionalized, while the unitary right, led by the National Action Party (PAN), has had more success in directing mass discontent against the PRI's corruption. Similarly in other countries undergoing profound socio-economic crises – Dominican Republic, Peru, Uruguay, Argentina, Brazil, etc – disunity on the left has weakened vital mass movements.

The Democratic Roots of Marxism

A major problem for Marxism is that it has an ambivalent theoretical legacy on the issue of democracy. Virtually all classical Marxists, including Marx, Engels and Lenin, had a profoundly democratic vision of the society that would emerge after the political revolution. But they did not lay out the principles or the concrete mechanisms by which the new society could move down the democratic path.

Karl Marx's writing left no doubt that he believed a classless, communist society could be achieved only if it were thoroughly democratic. He never dealt at length with how a democratic, communist society could be built, but based on the experiences of the Paris Commune in 1847 he did write about some of the features of a society of 'the people acting for itself, by itself'. Among the attributes of this type of society are: the abolition of standing permanent armies and their replacement by the armed people; no separation of legislative and executive functions; the end of state functionaries and bureaucracies, with the election of all officials, including judges, by universal suffrage; constant electoral control over the entire government with the right of recall; and the limitation of government wages to the level of those of workers as a whole in society.[3]

In *State and Revolution* Lenin discussed in detail the concept of the socialist government. Written in 1917 during the midst of the upheaval that led to the Bolshevik revolution, it argued that the dictatorship of the proletariat is the most democratic of all states, since it is the dictatorship of the majority. All the workers and their allies will participate in this society with only the enemies of the new state being excluded from participation. He called for the 'immediate break up [of] the old bureaucratic machine' and 'the construction of a new one which will enable us gradually to reduce all officialdom to naught', and in which the 'mass of the population will rise to participation'.

Lenin's famous essay has been labeled unrealistic and utopian. In fact it fails to address the hard issues such as what means should be used to deal with the opposition, and it does not even discuss the role of the party or the vanguard in the new society. By the time of his death in 1924, there are indications that Lenin had revised his view of the immediate democratic potential of the new society. He even admitted that Russia was a 'socialist state with a bureaucratic deformation'.[4]

With hindsight we can see some of the factors that have hindered the development of democracy in the Soviet Union and other revolutionary societies. The basic problem is that the global socialist revolution envisioned by Marx has not occurred. Furthermore no political revolution has taken place in any of the advanced capitalist countries. This means that the advanced imperialist countries have been able to mobilize their own extensive resources to impose huge costs upon societies attempting to move beyond capitalism.

These realities help explain why all the twentieth century social revolutions have tended to adopt rigid and non-democratic forms of the 'dictatorship of the proletariat'. In society after society we find the party and the state setting policy with only minimal consultation or participation from the masses. The specific mechanisms mentioned by Marx –

direct elections, the right of recall, the abolition of state functionaries, etc. – have been ignored. In most revolutionary countries, even after the imperialist challenge was met, the material needs of society and the drive for economic production led to a continued emphasis on centralization and the growth of a bureaucratic state. All this was compounded when the parties of these societies began to codify and put forth a reductionist or simplistic theory of the dictatorship of the proletariat, i.e. one which justified the concentration of power in the highest levels of the Communist party. This model was then adopted by most of the new revolutionary states in the third world, thereby perpetuating the growth of a deformed socialist state.

This critique of socialist development does not mean that there were not democratic tendencies at work. In some socialist countries a certain positive tension does exist between the democratic aspirations of the mass organizations and the authoritarian tendencies of the party and the state. Community associations, trade unions, women and youth organizations, etc. – these mass organizations provide a democratic content to many socialist societies. This explains why – with the notable exceptions of Hungary, Poland and Czechoslovakia in Eastern Europe, and the different experience of the Cultural Revolution in China – Communist governments have survived for decades without major upheavals.

No Communist state to date has established an authentic socialist democracy, an objective which Marx, Luxembourg, Lenin, Trotsky and other revolutionary leaders advocated. It is now imperative for revolutionary movements to take up the task of democratic socialist construction. This is the road that revolutionary parties in Latin America and in the United States will have to follow if they are to acquire legitimacy in the late twentieth century. And just as importantly, it is the only way to wage an effective ideological campaign against contemporary imperialism.

The New Revisionists

The democratic impasse faced by Marxism-Leninism is one factor that has led to the rise of what can be called the 'revisionist populist school' in Latin America and the United

States. Many supporters of this position are disillusioned revolutionaries of the 1960s and 1970s. Some were Maoists or Trotskyists, *foquistas* or Marxist-Leninists. Because of political defeats in the United States, Latin America and the Caribbean, these disillusioned activists now feel the need to break with the past, to look for totally new strategies and political formulas to challenge the existent order.

Although there is great diversity among those who hold these views, one can detect three political themes that run through the populist revisionist movement: 1) the belief that Marxism, Marxism-Leninism and the traditional concepts of the vanguard party and class analysis have been surpassed by the realities of the late twentieth century; 2) an almost romantic belief that the masses and mass movements are the only hope for the future; and 3) the belief that significant advances can be made by working within the capitalist system.[5]

In the United States these positions are reflected by the Democratic Socialists of America and the democratic management school. The former argues that it is possible for socialists to capture control of key political institutions in the United States like the Democratic party. The latter maintains that workers, by demanding participatory rights in the factory and by even buying control of companies, can begin to gain control of their lives.

Many other intellectuals and political activists, while not taking up the cause of revisionist populism, feel disillusioned with Marxism and adrift politically. They sense that the old political formulas and the language of the left are irrelevant, but they see no alternative on the horizon.

It is our position that the revisionist school and many other disillusioned leftists are right in their belief that it is time to discard the authoritarian and doctrinaire positions that derive from Maoism, Trotskyism and Marxism-Leninism. These tendencies are at the core of the sectarian political debates that tear apart the Marxist left throughout the world.

But the crisis of the 'isms' does not mean that Marxism and the body of revolutionary thought and practice that flows from it can simply be cast aside. The building blocks for a revolutionary movement are still found in this vital scientific tradition. The challenge we face as Marxists is to take these building blocks and apply them to the contemporary world. We desperately need new political strategies and formulas, but they must come out of the Marxist tradition.

The abandonment of Marxist concepts and categories by the new revisionists leads to two related flaws in the political program of the populist movement: 1) the lack of a clear class analysis, and 2) the lack of a strategic socialist vision. Instead of undertaking a systematic class analysis of society, the new populists postulate that there are two major social forces — the masses or the mass movements on the one hand, and the oligarchies or conservative ruling sectors on the other. For them the bourgeoisie and the working class cease to be the fundamental building blocks for analyzing society.

This lack of a clear class analysis begets the second flaw of the revisionists, the lack of a strategic socialist vision. By focusing on the masses and rejecting the need for a vanguard party, they in effect adopt a 'tailist position': they ignore the reality that the popular classes in the early stages of most struggles are almost inevitably influenced, if not dominated, by the values of the established order. In the United States for example, anti-communism is deeply ingrained in the public consciousness and will remain so for years to come. Any movement that wants to challenge the dominant order will have to deal with these mass attitudes, and it can only do so with strong leadership. It is this leadership that can forge a political vision and a program, not only by dealing with backward ideas in the movement, but also by handling internal social tensions within the movement itself. Without a Marxist analysis and a socialist agenda, these tensions and contradictions will almost inevitably lead to defeat or to cooptation by petit-bourgeois or even bourgeois reformist elements.

Pluralism in the Revolution

A starting point for developing a new democratic revolutionary project is the recognition that revolutionary struggle in itself is an explosive, democratizing force, regardless of whether it is led by reformists or socialists. In all revolutionary situations, the masses are rebelling against authoritarianism, repression, alienation, solitude, and atomization. They demand the opposite: fraternity, equality, solidarity and democracy. These basic demands and desires were evident in the French and American revolutions, in the popular upheaval in France in May 1968, and in the insurrectionary struggle in Nicaragua in 1978 to 1979. They were also fundamental themes of the social and political struggles that rocked the United States in the 1960s.

The mass movements that are born in these struggles are inherently participatory. The popular classes feel that their presence in a particular movement can make a difference and that they can change reality. This is participatory democracy in its most fundamental form. The individual identifies with the mass movement, thereby merging two opposing tendencies in contemporary societies. After the seizure of power this democratic impulse is all too frequently repressed or contained by the political leadership. In most twentieth-century socialist revolutions, the tendency has been to direct the revolutions' democratic impulses by setting up mass organizations that the state and the party ultimately control.

To reclaim the democratic revolutionary tradition, one must start by accepting two common criticisms of socialism. First, as we discussed above, most socialist countries do have authoritarian structures. Second, most vanguard political parties have been verticalist and undemocratic. To overcome these weaknesses the democratic principles enunciated by Marx and other revolutionary figures must be incorporated into a new concept of the vanguard, and applied in the very process of class struggle, both in the political and social revolutions. Clearly, there is a need for direction and guidance in any revolutionary process but this direction should help nurture and organize the democratic tendencies rather than repress them. To achieve this goal, anti-democratic tendencies in the vanguard parties must be changed.

One problem evolves from democratic centralism, the principle around which vanguard parties are organized. In theory it means that the base can influence and even participate in party decisions. But in practice democratic centralism often means that a small group of individuals run the organization from the top down. There is little room for authentic democratic discussion and participation.

A related problem is that in the different stages of struggle leading up to the political revolution there will be a need for a certain degree of secrecy and centralized decision-making because of the repressive nature of the state. But the need for secrecy and decision-making by the central committees has been overemphasized. Even more importantly, the tendencies towards secrecy and centralized decision-making have often crippled the basic drive for participation of the masses in the revolutionary movement. The new vanguard parties must be mass fronts in which the base has a direct role in deciding the direction and program of the party. Democracy will have to be integral to the advance and survival of the revolutionary movement.

Some of the most destructive features of democratic centralism manifested themselves in Grenada in 1983. The party leadership became so obsessed with its internal debate over the direction of the revolution that it split into two irreconcilable factions. Instead of turning to the masses to help resolve the dispute, an internecine struggle erupted in which one faction decided to physically eliminate the opposition, and opened a political chasm which Reagan exploited by invading the country. This marked the nadir of revolutionary movements in the Caribbean basin.

Well before the Grenadian catastrophe, the verticalist structure of most revolutionary parties had made them clearly vulnerable to charges by bourgeois ideologues and governments that Marxist-Leninist parties are by their very nature totalitarian and anti-democratic. One can, of course, argue over just how democratic bourgeois political parties are. But this evades the reality that in the advanced capitalist countries the masses by and large do believe that they live in democratic societies and that the dominant political parties respond to their interests. This belief can only be overcome if the revolutionary parties are able to demonstrate that their struggle is to expand the areas of democratic participation rather than to constrict them, and that their own political structures and programs are truly democratic. No political movement can emerge triumphant in the Americas – in the United States or in any Caribbean or Latin American country — unless the masses are convinced that their fundamental democratic rights will be advanced by a revolutionary movement.

The Democratic Impasse Under Capitalism

A major problem the left faces in the United States is the extent to which politics and political life have been separated from the daily life of the people. This tendency has been inherent in the evolution of capitalist societies since the time of the great bourgeois revolutions of the late eighteenth and early nineteenth century. In these revolutions, which were usually sparked by mass rebellions, the bourgeoisies took control of the state and set up institutions that channelled the mass movements into formal structures. Popular participation was limited to the ballot box, and certain sectors of the population, women, non-property owners, slaves, etc., were initially even disenfranchised.

Today, the bourgeois democracies, while having expanded the right to vote to include virtually all sectors of the population, have actually divorced democracy from the daily lives and concerns of the people. The centralization of economic power has gone hand in hand with the centralization of political power. Just as key economic decisions are made for the entire population in the corporate boardrooms, so also the key political decisions are made in the smoke-filled rooms of corporate political action committees and in corridors of power far removed from direct popular control. Watergate, and now Contragate, demonstrate how this drive towards the centralization of power, typically in the service of anti-communism, has created secret empires of near-dictatorial power.

Local issues and local participation become of decreasing importance as political power is concentrated at the national level. The people may have a final say at the ballot box over which party or group will hold power, but this comes only after the elites have drawn up programs and nominated candidates that are committed to preserving some variant of the status quo and to maintaining the power of the dominant economic interests. Election campaigns that cost millions are mounted to convince the electorate that one group or another can best serve their interests. These 'interests' are usually defined in terms of which party can produce the most rapid economic growth, interwoven with the 'politics of fear': fear of Communists taking over, fear of terrorists, or fear that our national security will be violated by some rebellious small country. Millions of people are misled into believing that these issues are decisive, even though the daily lives of the overwhelming majority are not affected in the least.

For Marxists, the existence of this ideological and political structure makes it extremely difficult to put forth a socialist agenda. Large sectors of the population, especially in the

United States, are alienated from politics; they correctly perceive that capitalist politics is an arena of competition between elites. This undermines the legitimacy of the capitalist system in the long term as millions disenfranchise themselves, not even bothering to vote. But this apathy also makes it difficult for revolutionary parties to build up support. These parties are viewed with suspicion by the population at large, as being little different from the bourgeois political parties. The left parties are viewed as continually debating 'irrelevant' political issues and as trying to sell or impose their ideas on others who are not interested. Moreover, the Marxist parties cannot even offer what the bourgeois parties do – more material goods and an improvement in the standard of living. These things, the public is told by Marxists, will come only after 'the revolution', when the wealth of the country will supposedly be divided up to satisfy everyone's needs. For the public at large, this is an abstract offer at best, and at worst it is seen as threatening the few economic benefits that some people have earned through their hard work.

To surmount these obstacles the revolutionary movements have to develop programs that begin to break down the artificial divide between politics and daily life that has been the hallmark of bourgeois democracies. To build national political organizations, the revolutionary parties have to first build by taking up local and grassroots issues. Cultural, social, and political issues must all be linked together on the local level.

Political Pluralism in the Vanguard

New national political movements of the left must be broadly based and pluralist in their political perspectives. Nothing will so quickly alienate any potential followers as a political party that insists upon developing the 'correct line', or engages in abstract political discussions of capitalism and socialism. Fortunately, in some countries a new pluralism in political perspectives is already emerging among the revolutionary movements, a pluralism that is innovative and democratizing. Marxist-Leninism is now only one current in the broader revolutionary process that exists in the third world and the industrialized countries. The historic dominance which Marxist-Leninists once held over revolutionary theory and practice has ended. Political pluralism within the vanguard and within the entire revolutionary movement is now on the agenda.

The two revolutions in the Americas – the Cuban and the Nicaraguan – demonstrated the shortcomings of orthodox Marxism-Leninism within the revolutionary movements. The 26th of July Movement, which seized power in Cuba in 1959, was in fact not a Marxist-Leninist party, nor were most of its leaders Marxist-Leninists, or even Marxists. It was only after two years of incessant US aggression and the consolidation of an alliance with the Soviet Union that the Cuban revolutionary leadership declared itself Marxist-Leninist. It is important to recognize that the Cuban vanguard, unlike many other parties in power, from the first day sought to incorporate other parties into the revolutionary process and to broaden popular participation.

The Cuban revolution was followed twenty years later by the Sandinista revolution which finally put to rest the claim of Marxist-Leninists that there is only one political philosophy that can lead to revolution. The revolutionary leadership in Nicaragua was comprised of Marxists, Marxist-Leninists, liberation theologists and radicalized social democrats. Few other successful revolutions have had such a pluralistic ideological leadership as the one that took power in Nicaragua. Images of Marx, Christ, Sandino, Lenin, Bolivar and José Santos Zelaya, (the president who was overthrown by the United States at the beginning of this century) are often seen side by side.

Today the positions of the Sandinista Front on national liberation, anti-imperialism, the mixed economy, political pluralism and non-alignment all reveal a broad ideological orientation. The revolutionary movement is multi-class, multi-ethnic, multi-doctrinal and politically pluralistic. And the party itself is not headed by a single strongman, but by a national directorate comprised of nine individuals who discuss the issues with broad input from the base before reaching agreements by consensus.

The government of Salvador Allende in Chile from 1970 to 1973 was also unique in that it marked the first time that a coalition of political parties tried to work together to establish a socialist society in the Americas. The effort failed, not because it was guided by a pluralistic coalition, but because the parties that comprised the Popular Unity government had no program for taking state power. They focused on using the limited executive power they held to carry out economic and social changes while doing little to control the military or the economic institutions dominated by the bourgeoisie. This error was rooted in the flawed historic analysis of the nature of Chilean democratic traditions, not in the multi-party composition of the Popular Unity government.

Throughout Latin America non Marxist-Leninist parties with a revolutionary content have emerged in recent years, such as the M–19 Movement in Colombia and the Workers Party (PT) in Brazil. In the United States, one can even point to the Jesse Jackson Rainbow coalition of 1984 as the first incipient effort to build a political organization that might someday have a revolutionary agenda.

The emerging political pluralism among the revolutionary movements reflects the political pluralism that already exists among the popular sectors. The masses of Latin America as well as the United States are extremely diverse – socially, economically and politically. It is only logical that they will have distinct political tendencies and programs and that different political parties will appeal to different social sectors. In countries like Chile, Colombia, and Peru, the existence of an array of left political parties makes it essential to build broad coalitions based on debate of revolutionary strategy and programs. At times this discussion will perhaps only be decided through the referenda in which the different revolutionary organizations compete.

The Nicaraguan Model

It is the need for a new democratic agenda that makes the Nicaraguan revolution such an important model. Although Nicaragua is a small, underdeveloped country, the course of its revolution provides insights and lessons for revolutionary movements throughout the Western Hemisphere. The Sandinista leadership has refused to declare it is Marxist-Leninist or that the country is undergoing a socialist revolution. Many outside observers see this as an effort to hide the real content of the revolution, to avoid giving the Reagan administration and other international opponents further grounds for attacking it. But the real reason for the refusal of the revolution to adopt a socialist nomenclature goes far deeper, involving: 1) the internal processes of the revolution, 2) its confrontation with imperialism, and 3) the general crisis of Marxism.

The starting point for understanding the ideological content of the Nicaraguan revolution is the declaration of the Sandinista Front in 1979 that the revolution is 'democratic, popular and anti-imperialist'. On one level this declaration is similar to proclamations made in the early stages of the revolutions in Russia and Cuba for example, where multi-class political fronts were set up. But in Nicaragua this phase of the revolution is being prolonged and deepened for two interrelated reasons. First, the challenge posed by Washington compels the revolutionary leadership to maintain the broadest possible system of class alliances. As one Nicaraguan revolutionary leader proclaimed: 'Our primary enemy is US imperialism. This defines the course of the revolution.'[6] Never in the history of twentieth century revolutionary struggles has such a small nation so close to the United States faced such prolonged and intense aggression as Nicaragua has. Nicaragua does not have the geographic defenses of being an island like Cuba, but has open borders and is surrounded by enemies. This is why it must appeal to all sectors of society, including the patriotic bourgeoisie, to participate in the struggle against imperialism.

The other central reason why Nicaragua has prolonged the 'democratic and popular' stage is because of the class structure of the Nicaraguan society. This was not a revolution of the working classes in the classical sense. In other revolutions, like those in Russia and Cuba, the proletariat was a much more important force. In Nicaragua the popular classes – the barrio residents, the artisans, the petty merchants, women, youth, the intellectuals, the petty bourgeoisie, etc. – were the driving force behind the revolution. The Sandinista Front itself reflects this reality. It is not a political party in which the working class is predominant. It is more of a mass front comprised of women, youth, peasant, professional and barrio organizations. Given this reality it is only logical for the Sandinista Front to focus on the democratic and popular content of the revolution.[7]

Related to these social and political realities is the crisis of socialism. Marxism-Leninism has lost much of its appeal due to the non-democratic and authoritarian nature of many revolutions. The Sandinista leadership is aware of this crisis, and that in part explains why the Front has shunned any labels that would place it firmly in the Marxist-Leninist tradition. Nor has there been any premeditated strategy of moving through the classic stages of a socialist revolution — only a fundamental anti-imperialist stance, a realization of the limits the class structure of Nicaraguan society imposes on the revolution, and a pragmatic recognition that in order to have legitimacy the revolution must be democratic and have a popular base.

This position is re-enforced by the fact that many of the Sandinista Front's members were part of the broader political movement of the 1960s and 1970s in which many experienced disillusionment with traditional and doctrinaire Marxist formulations. Some militants in the *Frente* had actually been members of Maoist, Trotskyist and other Marxist-Leninist organizations. The split of the *Frente* into three tendencies in 1977 was in part due to the effort to move away from the traditional formulas and to come up with a viable program responding to Nicaragua's needs. In a year and a half they reunited, but on a program that reflected a broader, more open approach to revolutionary struggle.

The refusal to label the revolution Socialist or Marxist-Leninist does not mean, however, that socialist and Marxist analyses are not at the core of the political program of the Sandinista Front. As members of the National Directorate themselves explain: 'Any revolution will, at some point, have to break with the capitalist path. All the theoreticians agree that capitalism is destined to be superceded by a system of production and a way of life that can only be characterized as socialist.' (Jaime Wheelock). Since 'the only socialism is scientific socialism' (Victor Tirado), it is not surprising that 'insofar as doctrine is concerned we are primarily guided by the scientific theory that is Marxism' (Humberto Ortega).[8]

Indeed, Marxist categories – like the bourgeoisie, the proletariat, the vanguard, collectivization, and imperialism — frame the internal political analysis of the *Frente* and the evolution of its political program. The genius of the *Frente* is that it has fused Marxism with Sandinismo, the revolutionary nationalist tradition of the country.

These factors help explain why the Nicaraguan revolution has responded to internal and external challenges, not by declaring a dictatorship of the proletariat, as previous revolutions have done, but by broadening its democratic content.⁹ This approach is evident in every major crisis the revolution has faced. It was first demonstrated in May, 1980, when the pro-bourgeois forces, led by junta member Alfonso Robelo, pressed for non-Sandinista organizations to have a majority in the newly created Council of State, a body with legislative powers. The Sandinista Front rejected these pressures and responded by appointing representatives of the mass organizations to the Council instead. This caused sectors of the bourgeoisie, including Robelo, to pull out of the government. But more importantly it marked the beginning of a process that has led to an ever expanding role for the mass organizations in the government.

At another major turning point, shortly after the US invasion of Grenada in 1983, the role of the popular classes was again expanded. The National Directorate adopted the slogan 'All Arms to the People' and began distributing over 200,000 arms to the militias and popular organizations around the country. Today, one out of every five inhabitants of the country is armed: this gives real power to the masses and it means that to keep their loyalty, the *Frente* has to directly involve them in all aspects of the revolution.

The debate over autonomy for the indigenous communities of the Atlantic Coast illustrates how democracy and the right to self determination have shaped the Sandinista revolution. The FSLN, after learning from its initial mistakes with the Miskitos (the largest Indian group on the coast), is succeeding in bringing non-revolutionary ethnic communities into the process through extensive discussions of their interests and needs. Autonomy is a principle incorporated into the country's new constitution, and specific political and economic institutions are being set up to insure that minorities on the Atlantic Coast have control of their lives and their societies. In the face of expedient separatist sentiment stirred up in large part by the USA, the Sandinista Front has made major strides in dealing with the issue of autonomy and self-determination among minorities. To a great degree, the ability of the government to incorporate the ethnic minorities is made possible by the commitment of the Nicaraguan revolution to democracy and full participation of all social and ethnic groups.

Perhaps the clearest example of how a certain revolutionary pragmatism has enabled Nicaragua to make qualitative advances along the democratic road is found in the elections of 1984. When in early 1984 the National Directorate decided to hold national elections that year – honoring a previctory commitment one sector of the *Frente* viewed them as a fairly formal procedure that meant little for the development of the revolution. But once the commitment to instead engage in fair and open elections had been made, an internal dynamic was set in motion that compelled the entire Front to take the elections seriously and to expand the country's democratic processes. The mass organizations of the revolution, and particularly the Committees for the Defense of the Revolution, launched a program of dialogue and internal education that significantly raised popular consciousness around political and economic issues. As a result, the *Frente* won a resounding victory in the midst of a counterrevolutionary war and a deteriorating economy. The elections demonstrated how a revolutionary government can solidify its hold on power, not by adopting increasingly dictatorial measures, but by building mass democratic support.

The deepening of the Nicaraguan agrarian reform constitutes another major step in the democratizing process. Land pressures, particularly in the war zones, led many campesinos in 1984 and 1985 to demand the expropriation of state farms as well as large private holdings. Rather than try to contain these demands by pushing for state-run production cooperatives, the *Frente* decided to distribute land titles to the peasantry. In the countryside, this was a recognition of the basic rights of the rural inhabitants to organize their communities and their lives in the way they wanted.

The adoption of the new constitution in 1986 marked yet another significant step forward in the Nicaraguan democratic process. Drafted by the constituent assembly that was elected in 1984, the document was submitted in early 1986 to the country for discussion. To facilitate these discussions, a series of *cabildos abiertos*, or town meetings, were held in communities around the country in which the populace and the mass organizations made suggestions for changes in the constitution. Almost immediately the mass organizations made known in these sessions their discontent with some of the political institutions proposed in the draft constitution. One particular complaint was that the constitution called for a single elective assembly in which only representatives of political parties could be represented. A very interesting proposal was put forth for the establishment of a bicameral legislature in which one body would be a popular assembly with the mass organizations represented, while the other would contain popularly elected representatives from the political parties. Only after much debate was this proposal rejected.

In sum the first steps on the road to socialist democracy are being taken in Nicaragua. This is not to say that the country is by any means an ideal democratic state: it has serious limitations, among them an entrenched and inefficient bureaucracy, a scarcity of trained and educated militants, and above all, a lack of democratic traditions. All these factors help explain why some of the authoritarian tendencies that have characterized previous revolutions are also seen in Nicaragua. But the momentum is decisively in a democratic direction and this has deepened the meaning of democracy, not only for Nicaragua, but for the rest of the Americas as well.[10]

The Democratic Building Block

The Nicaraguan experience enables us to begin to lay out some of the building blocks for the formation of an authentic socialist democracy. Such a democracy must have two fundamental goals: 1) the end of social and economic inequalities, and 2) the full participation of the population in the political and economic life of the country. These basic objectives can only be achieved by creating a political system that provides for consultative, participatory and representative democracy. It is essential to recognize that democracy limited to the political party system is not democracy at all. It must instead permeate all aspects of civil society. Democratic practices must prevail in union, cultural and religious organizations (for believers and non-believers alike); in community activities, education and even international relations.

The components of consultative and participatory democracy are well known in many socialist societies. They involve the formation and development of distinct mass organizations for the workers, the peasantry, teachers, youth, women, and so on. Participatory democracy also means that many of these organizations should have substantial responsibilities in the workplace: in the factory, the field, the office and the school. Social and economic equality can only be achieved if the workers (broadly defined) play a role in running the economic and bureaucratic institutions that affect their lives.

The other democratic form, that of representative democracy, has until recently been largely the preserve of bourgeois democracies. But representative democracy must become a central part of the political life of socialist societies if authoritarian tendencies are to be avoided. As in Nicaragua, the national leaders of the country should be elected by the direct vote of the people with a variety of candidates and political parties participating. The representatives of the legislative assemblies, or parliaments must also be elected through a similar process.

In the arena of representative democracy there should be one fundamental break with the bourgeois system – the mass organizations must be allocated a role in the political system that is independent of the political parties. The granting of representation to these organizations in a popular assembly is the most direct way in which the institutions of participatory democracy are merged with those of representative democracy.

The most difficult challenge for revolutionary socialist societies may be the development of a pluralist system involving competing political parties. As was stated earlier, in most revolutions there will be no single vanguard party but a variety of revolutionary parties, each with a somewhat different agenda for constructing a socialist society. These parties will have to devise political or electoral mechanisms for debating their different views in public so that the specific direction the society takes can be decided by the entire body politic. And if there is to be public debate and elections, this also implies that the political parties will have to have access to the mass media. Each political party will need its own newspaper, its own printing press, its own bookstores and reading rooms as well as equal access to radio and TV.

The existence of political pluralism among the revolutionary parties also raises the question of what role non-revolutionary parties may have in a socialist society. Should the political system and the 'rules of the political game' be set up to marginalize any party that is not fully committed to the basic program of the revolution the tendency would be to say that non-revolutionary parties should be excluded since their

Socialism and Democracy 61

objective is to undermine the construction of a communist society.

But if this is the case, it raises the question of who defines which parties are revolutionary and which are not? Given the hegemonic position of the revolutionary parties in any socialist democracy, it will be to the advantage of the entire society to allow any party to play a role. This will provide an escape valve for the more discontented elements, and simultaneously serve as a political barometer for the revolutionary parties to make adjustments in their course if the non-revolutionary parties gain momentum. The bourgeois democracies, when they feel secure, have allowed Marxist parties to compete in their elections, and there is no reason why non-revolutionary parties should be excluded in a vibrant and dynamic socialist society.[11]

3

The Neglected Revolutionary Allies

In most countries in the Americas, those bent on transforming the existent social order are confronted by the chasm that exists between the social and mass movements on the one hand and revolutionary political formations on the other. It is in the United States where this dichotomy is perhaps the most glaring with Marxist parties being almost totally excluded from the country's political life. But this dichotomy also exists throughout Latin America and the Caribbean, including the three largest countries – Argentina, Brazil and Mexico. What explains this divergence between the masses and Marxism? Why do most popular struggles – whether women or Black movements in the United States, or the recent popular struggles that forced out military regimes in Argentina, Uruguay and Brazil – have little or no links to revolutionary political formations?[1]

A central problem is the failure of Marxism to explain the social and political transformations that have taken place in capitalist societies. The fundamental political strategy of most Marxism-Leninism has changed little since the time of the Bolshevik Revolution – they still maintain that revolutions are to be led in the third world by the worker-peasant alliance, or in the developed countries by the workers, with perhaps a secondary role for the farmers. To move beyond this limiting framework, we need to distinguish between the class position of a particular group and the actual politico-ideological orientation of that group. In the process of building a revolutionary movement it is not sufficient to know simply the class structure of a society; we must also understand the political and ideological views that the different strata hold. For example, it is not as important to know if bank employees are part of the working class that produces 'surplus value' as it is to know what political attitudes – real or potential – they hold vis-a-vis the established order.[2] In other words we cannot evaluate the revolutionary potential of any group until we have considered its political orientation as well as its position in the class structure.

As the first chapter demonstrated, the proletariat in the early part of this century did have a politico-ideological orientation which made it an extremely dynamic social force. It played a central role in the founding of most of the Communist parties, and in the 1930s this class posed a serious challenge to the dominant capitalist order. The peasantry in Latin America was also an explosive force for many decades, often sparking major revolts against the established regimes. But in recent decades the most dynamic political sector in many societies has not been the working class, but a broad social grouping comprised of heterogeneous sectors of society which we call the third force. Today, this is a pivotal force; it can spark revolutionary movements and help lead them.

The third force is not a new class, or even a single consolidated class. It is comprised of a number of diverse social groups and social movements that are defined more by their social and political attributes than by their relationship to the work-place. Some sectors of the third force, such as women and ethnic movements, actually have a multi-class composition. What makes them organizable around progressive or even radical political programs, is the discrimination and oppression they experience in the general social structure. This oppression can have direct repercussions in the workplace. Most women and Blacks for example, because of their status in US society, are paid inferior wages; but the origin of their exploitation is in the evolution of capitalist society as a whole, i.e. in the totality of social and class structures.

The political importance of the third force does not negate the fact that the working class will always be at the core of any revolutionary process – it is the historic subject of all popular revolutions. As Marx proclaimed over a century ago it is the proletariat, the very antithesis of the bourgeoisie, that will ultimately end the hegemony of the capitalist class. Because of its position in society, it alone can be the central social force in building a socialist society. But in the seizure of power and in the first stages of transition, the working class in virtually all societies cannot move forward unless broad class alliances are forged with other social sectors. These sectors need to be won over for the triumph of the political revolution; their continued support and involvement are also necessary for the social revolution to begin to build a classless socialist society.

The Composition of the Third Force

It is important to analyze the composition of the social movements and the diverse social sectors that comprise the third force to understand their potential for incorporation in the struggle for socialism. Naturally the composition of the third force will vary from country to country, and particularly between the developed and the underdeveloped countries. Below we will discuss three general categories of the third force and their relative importance in different social formations:

1. The Middle Class, Intellectuals and the Petit Bourgeoisie

Perhaps the largest grouping in this category are the salaried 'middle classes' of the private and public sectors. This includes employees of the state bureaucracies, the lower strata of the technocracy, the office clerks who work in corporations or small businesses, and the professional workers in health and educational institutions (teachers, nurses, etc.). In the United States they are often called white-collar workers. In the third world these workers are closely tied to the state bureaucracies and are concentrated in the cities.

Intellectuals of all types are part of this category, including writers, university professors, artists, students of all levels, intellectuals and members of policy or research organizations. Although relatively small in numbers, they are key in the development of any society because of their role in developing culture and ideology.

This category also includes the petty bourgeoisie, or the small independent business people who do not identify with either the interests of the workers or with those of large capitalist businesses. In the third world the petty bourgeoisie is more open to revolutionary agendas than in the developed countries because in the third world many small business interests are threatened by the advance of monopoly capital.

2. The Economically Marginalized Sectors of Society

The residents of urban slums who are unemployed or only marginally employed form a very distinctive component of the third force. In the third world these people live in the *barrios* (Mexico), the *flavelas* (Brazil), the *callampas* (Chile) or the *pueblos jovenes* (Peru). Women who live in these slums as the heads of households are sometimes potentially very militant, since they are the first who feel scarcities and the high cost of living. This sector also includes artisans and many small merchants who are often part of what is called the 'informal sector'. They engage in a variety of merchandising or petty-entrepreneurial activities, ranging from street vending to running cottage industries.

The marginalized sector also includes people of all social origins in both the developed and underdeveloped countries who are denied social services such as water, electricity, streets, or welfare benefits. In the United States, the large numbers of people who struggle to survive on their social security benefits or who depend on desultory social programs for their survival constitute a large, marginalized strata of society. If politically mobilized they could be an explosive social force. To their ranks one also might add increasingly marginalized family farmers, driven into bankruptcy by overproduction and high interest rates.

3. The Social Movements

The great social struggles of the past quarter-century have been waged over broad social issues that generally transcend the workplace: civil rights, gender equality, opposition to nuclear power and environmental degradation, peace, the right to housing (squatters movements throughout Latin

America), and so on. In almost every case the leadership, and most of the social impetus, for these struggles have come from the 'third force', outside the traditional unions or working-class political parties. Part of the reason for the importance of the third force is the changing nature of the working class itself and the weakening of traditional forms of organization. In the 1930s, the US working class was both militant and hegemonic as the industrial unions of the CIO fought not only for decent wages and union recognition, but for a broad agenda of social demands ranging from civil rights to public housing. But today these sectors are neither as militant nor as sweeping in their vision. The leaderships of the unions have become thoroughly bureaucratized, while the decline of basic manufacturing and unionized transportation has weakened those sectors which have played the most progressive roles. Put on the defensive by massive capital restructuring and a relentless bosses' offensive, union leaderships are limiting their efforts to the conservative strategy of protecting their remaining jobs. Not only have they made concession after concession, but they have generally lost the nerve to attack the real, structural causes of plant closure and job flight.

The same phenomena can be seen in the Latin American labor movements. The trade unions with a long history tend to be more moderate and less combative. In Peru for example the older unions dominated by the APRA or the Communist Party are not as militant as new sectors of the working class. This is also true of Chile where the copper miners who have been organized for decades tend to be more conservative than others. The third force can help break this impasse within the working class by raising broader social issues. Its very dynamism can ignite other sectors that have been demobilized and depoliticized. Perhaps the most distinctive constituency of the third force are radicalized Christians.

In the Americas, Christians have been polarized by social revolution. On one side stands the fundamentalist New Right, a principal support of Reaganism, together with the reactionary wing of the Catholic hierarchy. On the other side are new communities of religious activists, ranging from the progressive Black churches of the United States to the Catholic *communidades de base* in Latin America. In many countries Christians and Marxists are forging a common front against exploitation, oppression, imperialism, even capitalism. Each side contributes its accumulated social experience. The churches, in particular, have dynamic grassroots relationships, through the parishes, with those sections of the working classes outside the trade unions or classical organizations of the left. The religious left also brings its own developing ideology, Liberation Theology, which unites traditional spiritual values with advocacy of revolutionary change to end the exploitation of the poor.

Marxists, on the other hand, bring to this common front an analysis which pinpoints the origins of exploitation and oppression in specific economic and political structures, and a strategy which outlines the broad course of necessary social transformation. As the struggle unfolds Marxists attempt to organize popular constituencies in a systematic fashion, often in underground networks, to resist the terrorism of the state. Local parishes and Christian organizations have increasingly played vital roles in structuring this counter-society of the oppressed.

In Latin America literally tens of thousands of Christians have joined revolutionary movements ranging from urban political coalitions to rural guerrilla fronts. Meanwhile in the United States religious activists have provided the key network that holds together the solidarity movements with Central America and Southern Africa. Exposure to the socio-economic realities of the hemisphere has also sharpened the domestic politics of US religious activists. One landmark was the 1986 declaration of the US Catholic Bishops Conference which pointedly condemned Reaganomics and embraced the cause of the poor and the unemployed.

The Third Force in Nicaragua

In the Sandinista Revolution the third force played a central role in the insurrectionary climax and it has been deeply involved in the subsequent social transformations. The FSLN incorporated not only the workers and peasants in the insurrectional project, but also all those sectors here considered to belong to the third force, particularly slum dwellers, students and the youth.

Although the armed struggle was initially based in the mountains, and drew heavily on the peasantry for support, as had Sandino fifty years before, by the mid–1970s the movement had expanded to include the urban masses in the cities. Together with workers, students, youth, Christians, housewives, teachers, nurses, civil servants, professionals, small and medium producers were all brought into the struggle as it advanced. Furthermore, in the final stages the popular character expanded to include a broad policy of alliances with even the patriotic sectors of the bourgeoisie.[3]

On the ideological front, the FSLN's program upheld the values of liberty, social justice, democracy, human dignity, and the nation's right to self determination. These values cut across class lines and had a particularly strong appeal to the third force, which assumed an increasingly pivotal role as the revolutionary movement advanced. The FSLN took class struggle to all corners and levels of society without any class prejudices. The demand for democracy, nationalism, and the joy of living and sharing was not left to the bourgeoisie, to the Protestant sects, or to the Lions Club. There was a drive to politicize all aspects of everyday life and to humanize the political tasks. This struggle transformed social relations and values, especially among those with social origins in the third force. For those fighting in the armed movement the very nature of human relationships changed: they could break free from the drab and confining life of the established order, from family selfishness, from the routine of dull uninteresting days, and from the daily commercialization of their lives.

The seizure of political power did not end the revolution's need to win mass support. This support had to be continually nurtured and developed, not through the vertical imposition of state police, but by responding to mass needs and interests. Today the specific interests of every class and social group are represented at the local, regional and national levels. Similarly, the harshness of the tasks imposed by the counterrevolution and US military aggression has not eliminated such joyful activities as sports, music festivals, and parties after combat or work. The Sandinista Revolution demonstrates that the struggle for socialism can mobilize the majority of people in the tasks of representative and participatory democracy. It also shows the revolutionary potential of the different sectors of the third force, even in conditions of material underdevelopment such as those left to Nicaraguan society by Somoza.

Costa Rica

Costa Rica illustrates the opposite tendency – how the bourgeoisie can manipulate and capture the third force. By playing on the nationalism of the Costa Ricans and the pride they feel in their parliamentary system (which they consider exceptional among the countries of Central America), the bourgeoisie has been able to turn the populace against the Sandinista government in Nicaragua, and against any domestic movement with a revolutionary agenda. In particular, the manipulation of government bureaucrats, teachers and health workers has enabled the Costa Rican bourgeoisie to influence and dominate the urban masses. The role of US cultural penetration in this process has also been important. It has facilitated the implantation of consumerist values among the middle sectors through the press, radio, television and the school system. As a result, Costa Rica is the country in Central America, with the possible exception of Panama, most permeated by US values.

Until now, the leftist parties and movements in Costa Rica have given little attention and importance to the social sectors of the third force, leaving them to the bourgeoisie or to reformist groups that are directly or indirectly supportive of the bourgeoisie. The left over the years has been active in the worker's movement in Costa Rica, especially on the banana plantations, but it has devoted little attention to the urban middle classes and the petty bourgeoisie. In Costa Rica the revolutionary organizations have failed to recognize that the third force cannot be won over by using the same ideological or political appeal that is used with the peasantry or the working class.

However, Costa Rica does have a rich legacy of experiences on which to build a new revolutionary movement. In the past many social sectors, particularly those linked to the third force, have been involved in progressive and even revolutionary movements. Broad popular support made possible the 1948 revolution led by Pepe Figueres which ushered in a period of social reform and progress. In the 1970s students, teachers and state workers supported major strikes by banana and rural workers. In the late 1970s, many social sectors and even centrist political parties provided direct support to the Sandinista Front in its fight to overthrow the Somoza regime. It's no accident that today the United States and the conservative political parties have launched a campaign within Costa Rica's important urban middle sectors against the Sandinista government, accusing it of 'communist totalitarianism', hoping thereby to wipe out any public sympathy that may exist for the revolutionary government in Managua.[4]

Chile

Sectors of the third force were a critical battleground during the Chilean Popular Unity government from 1970 to 1973. The left had particularly strong support among teachers, students, artists and intellectuals. But other parts of the middle class, and virtually the entire petty bourgeoisie, were lost to the Christian Democrats. This was the weak link of the Chilean political process which the bourgeoisie and US imperialism exploited to the hilt. The *gremios*, which included business and professional organizations as well as truck drivers, were especially dangerous. They served as the shocktroops of the counterrevolution, as was demonstrated by the truckers' strike which crippled the economy in 1972.

The political parties of the Popular Unity were also weak in encouraging the new social movements. For example, they did very little work around feminist issues, limiting themselves largely to organizing women around traditional class issues. The vacuum which resulted was exploited by the right — as exemplified by the 'pots and pans movement' in which housewives, particularly in the middle- and upper-class areas of Santiago, banged on their pots and pans throughout the nights to protest the alleged food shortages caused by the Allende government. Although few working-class women participated in the pots and pans movement, the fact remained that Popular Unity offered little political space for women to organize and mobilize around their own issues. By contrast, the Christian Democratic opposition had a strong base among women; it embodied certain middle-class values that can be liberating for women in traditional male dominated societies. In all the elections held in Chile from 1970 to 1973, women from *all* social classes consistently voted in higher percentages than men for the Christian Democrats and other anti-socialist parties.

The 1970 to 1973 period in Chile also demonstrated the

right's ability to wage war on the ideological front, particularly its adroit use of the mass media. Through television, the radio and newspapers like *El Mecurio*, the reactionary parties worked incessantly to inflame the middle class against the government. The values of 'democracy' and 'anti-Communism' were at the center of the media campaign against Allende.

For years after the military coup, the petty bourgeoisie as well as the bourgeoisie remained loyal to the Pinochet regime. The military provided them with economic benefits by driving down the wages of the working class and by allowing a wide array of up-scale consumer goods to be brought into the country with virtually no import duties. But by the early 1980s the economy was in serious trouble. As unemployment rose and industry after industry was plagued by bankruptcy, the petty bourgeoisie and even sectors of the bourgeoisie turned against the government. Massive demonstrations rocked the country from 1983 to 1985, threatening the stability of the regime itself.

The key issue is whether the left can now capture some of these discontented middle sectors, who will otherwise support alternatives put forth by the Christian Democrats and those sectors of the bourgeoisie that now oppose Pinochet. A key to this process is the projection of a vision and a new set of values that captures the imagination of the middle sectors. Democracy is the central value. Given the unconditional support the Chilean bourgeoisie has provided to the dictatorial regime for almost a decade it is in an unparalleled weak position. The left is already taking advantage of the situation. It is pushing for broad participation in the struggle and has gained momentum within the working class, the universities and the *poblaciones* or shanty towns that ring the city of Santiago. Through its unconditional and consistent advocacy of democratization the left is opening a new wedge between Pinochet and the middle strata.[5]

Peru

The Peruvian case demonstrates the strategic role that the new social forces can play in a pre-revolutionary situation when the left is cognizant of their importance. In the 1970s, the Peruvian left, part of which originated in the guerrilla and student movements of the 1960s, focused on building a base in the traditional working class. But this strategy came into question after the failure of the general strikes of 1977 to 1978. It was then that the left realized that the workers in the 'formal' sectors constituted only 14% of the laborforce in the country, and that only half of those workers were unionized.

The left then began to focus more on the *barrios jovenes*, the poor urban areas that were filled with people coming to Lima looking for jobs and a better life. The left agitated with the barrio people to demand water, streets, electricity and health care. Soup kitchens and womens' educational programs were started, while basic skill workshops were set up in many neighborhoods. As a result of this work, the left began to tap the explosive social energy of the barrios. The barrios, even more than the workers in the factories, have the capacity to shut down Lima. The barrio residents have taken to the streets on different occasions, burning tires, shutting down traffic, and generaly halting commerce within the city. Moreover, these barrio uprisings invariably capture widespread media attention, making the demands of the left visible on a national scale.

The work in the barrios and with other social sectors has made the left a major force on the Peruvian political scene. In the 1985 presidential elections, the United Left political coalition came in second, behind APRA and Alan García, but well ahead of the country's right-wing political parties. This marks the first time anywhere in Latin America that the left has made such a strong political showing since the early 1970s. Today the left in Peru has some of the best political strategists in all of Latin America, many of whom have their social roots in the third force, particularly the universities and schools.

Teachers and Sendero Luminoso

Teachers have been a particularly important force in Peru. Their numbers mushroomed in the 1960s as the Alliance for Progress and the first government of Fernando Belaúnde Terry, from 1963 to 1968, placed a heavy emphasis on education as the way to modernize the country. As a result teachers and schools were established for the first time in many rural communities, and the local teacher often became one of the most prestigious and important community leaders. The teachers' movement became a progressive current in Peruvian society, with the left developing a particularly strong base. In fact the largest guerrilla movement today, the Sendero Luminoso, focused on building its cadre among the teachers in the 1970s. Using the university in Ayacucho as its base, it reached many of the young teachers who were being trained, incorporating them into its ranks, and sending them out into rural communities as teachers to organize and recruit for Sendero Luminoso.

While displaying a particular genius for using teachers to build their movement around the country, the leadership of the Sendero Luminoso does not display an agility to forge a political program that draws in other sectors of the middle class or the urban working class. Its efforts to organize a particular social sector, the Indians, has led the party to develop a platform that is anti-technological and even anti-industrial. The mistake of the Sendero Luminoso lies in its failure to recognize that a revolutionary movement must build a new society that appeals to sectors of the third force as well as to the workers and the Indians.[6]

El Salvador

The Salvadoran movement today demonstrates the pivotal importance of the third force. In many ways the FMLN has shown particular agility in drawing in the middle sectors to support what is a profoundly revolutionary program. Over the years teachers and government workers have been in the forefront of the movement, as have the base church communities, which are part of the third force. The massive insurrectionary movement from 1979 to 1981 demonstrated the social breadth of this mobilization, incorporating large numbers of people from the middle classes as well as from the barrios and the working class. Only the brutal repression of the state contained this mass movement. Today the very existence of the Democratic Revolutionary Front (FOR), demonstrates the success the left has had in attracting social democratic and even Christian Democratic sectors that are primarily rooted in the middle class. However, if one sector of the third force remains a weak link for the FMLN, it is the petty bourgeois business and merchant sectors. By and large the oligarchy and the industrial bourgeoisie maintain the support of this class. Its representatives play key roles in rightwing and centrist political parties, especially Duarte's Christian Democrats. This is a major stumbling block for the FMLN, one that will be difficult to overcome.

Recently, the five politico-military organizations that comprise the FMLN have begun to form a single political party that will be formally Marxist-Leninist. This represents an important step, but one that raises questions about the new party's relationship to the third force. This new political party gives no indication of making the errors and mistakes that were committed by many of the orthodox Marxist-Leninist parties in Latin America. Clearly, the FMLN is committed to a liberation struggle against the Salvadoran bourgeoisie and the United States. In this sense, the FMLN has more in common with the 26th of July Movement in Cuba and the Sandinista Front in Nicaragua than it does with many of the Communist parties of the past.[7]

The United States

In the United States, the third force is more influential than in any other country in the Americas. Large in numbers, it is decisive in determining the political consciousness of society as a whole. Historically, it has provided leadership for a gamut of progressive movements and today it is the social force most capable of building a new consciousness leading to profound change. But the third force has an ambiguous legacy in the United States. In the 1960s and early 1970s it was at the center of the social and political upheaval that gripped the country. The Black and womens' movements, the youth rebellion, the environmental and anti-nuclear campaigns, and the gay rights movement – these were all led and/or composed of social sectors from the third force. It provided the momentum that tore apart the cold war consensus and the oppressive social conservatism of the early postwar era.

Today, however, it is clear that most of these movements are at an impasse, or even in decline, as the New Right has seized control of the political and social agendas in the United States. What happened? Why are these movements on the defensive after being in the political forefront? Two interrelated problems have plagued most of these groups: 1) the disunity and separatism among the different social movements and single issue campaigns, and 2) their inability to develop a political program in conjunction with the working class.

Their disunity is due to the very diversity of the movements that are part of the third force. Women, Blacks, and gays for example all view themselves as suffering particular forms of social oppression that have to be rectified separately, while the single issue movements, like the environmental and anti-nuclear campaigns, believe that they cannot let their movements or issues be diluted by others. And behind most of these movements is a fundamental distrust of authority and centralized organization. These forms of control are usually considered anti-democratic and are often identified with the very forces of domination and oppression that they are struggling against.

A related problem is the general enmity that exists between the different sectors of the third force and the working class, particularly the white working class and its bureaucratized union leadership. In the 1960s and early 1970s, these differences were particularly virulent as the youth and anti-war movements accused the white working class of being pro-war and socially conservative, while the workers responded that the anti-war protesters were arrogant 'bums' and social misfits who couldn't do an honest day's work. These antagonisms assumed even more ominous dimensions when the white working class felt besieged by the Black and women's movements which demanded equal employment opportunities, and an end to most white male privileges.

These divisions and antagonisms were exploited with a vengeance by the New Right. In the 1970s conservatives began to build systematically on the white backlash against the social movements. And they also had the genius to realize that some of the same social strata that the New Left drew upon – particularly the middle class and the upwardly mobile petty bourgeoisie – could be mobilized and serve the New Right. The result was the birth of an array of reactionary social movements with a populist base, such as the right to life movement, the anti-busing and anti-tax campaigns, and the born-again Christian and fundamentalist churches. These movements, with heavy financial support from the nouveaux riches and the bourgeoisie (particularly from the Southern and Western states), were able to build a social base and to develop a national political movement that catapulted Ronald Reagan into the presidency.

For almost a decade now, the progressive social movements and the political remnants of the New Left have been fighting a largely unsuccessful reaguard battle to stem the assault of the New Right on many of the gains that they won in the 1960s and 1970s. A sense of drift and powerlessness now grips not only the progressive social movements but also broad sectors of the US populace including farmers, the working poor and the unemployed and homeless.

However the assault of the New Right and the implementation of its economic program, which favours the wealthy and the privileged at the expense of the poor, has created objective conditions that could potentially lead to the birth of new social and political opposition movements. It is even feasible that some sectors of the white working class and the lower middle class could be incorporated into this process.

Income distribution figures reveal that a bell jar economy is taking hold in the United States, not unlike that of many third world countries. The poor in the last decade have gotten poorer while the rich under the auspices of Reaganomics have become dramatically richer. Members of the broad middle class apart from highly paid professionals (like doctors, computer technicians, or plant managers) have more often than not been pushed downward on the social and economic ladder. At the same time, the trade union movement has been put under siege as industries like airline and trucking are 'deregulated' (thereby driving down wage levels) while basic industries like steel are gutted as production is internationalized. The new 'growth industries' in the USA are now the non-union, minimum wage service sectors, like the fast food chains. More workers are now employed by MacDonalds than by the steel industry. Today only 15 per cent of the US private sector workforce is unionized, a figure that is lower than that of some Latin American countries.

The basic problem is, of course, that the economic and political assault of the New Right demoralizes these groups and makes it difficult for them to organize. The one glimmer of hope on the national level in recent years has been the formation of the Rainbow Coalition under Jesse Jackson. It has brought together many of the leaders and activists of the old social movements, and it has built a mass base, particularly among the poor and exploited in the Black and third world communities.

But the key to the revival of a progressive movement does not rest simply in whether or not it can field a major presidential candidate, or incorporate some of its agenda into the Democratic platform. Political debate on the national level is important, but even more important is the very existence of a national organization and the commitment of its different social and political components to wage a struggle in the heart of civil society. Like the New Right, any new progressive movement will have to wage a protracted struggle in the institutions that shape society – the media, the universities, in the home, churches, trade unions, and the wide range of local social organizations (like parent-teacher associations) that are part of day to day life at the community level.

In the campaign within civil society, a page can be taken out of the work of the solidarity movements around Central America and South Africa. In the very midst of the Reagan era, they have conducted campaigns in the churches, the schools and the media that have successfully mobilized broad sectors of public opinion against Reagan's interventionist policies. It should also be remembered that the successes of the New Left and civil rights movements in the 1960s and 1970s were not due to victories on the national electoral level they were defeated in major elections, as the presidential campaigns of 1968 and 1972 demonstrate); rather it was the New Left's assault on the very infrastructure of US society — the media, the universities, the corporations, and the traditional patriarchal family – that led to upheaval and change.

Today, the third force, in conjunction with the new impoverished sectors of the working class, has the potential to wage a much more sophisticated and effective battle within civil society, not only to open up new vistas and to generate new values, but also to resist the new forms of social and economic oppression that the Reagan administration is implanting in the workplace as well as the home. If the Rainbow Coalition can incorporate this kind of strategy, then it might eventually be in a position to carry out some of the profound changes in US political structures that eluded the New Left.

The Weak Links in Bourgeois Rule

What are the weak links in the chain of bourgeois rule?

Where can breakthroughs be made? One weakness is that the bourgeoisie, and the capitalist system it controls, are driven to produce an ever increasing materialistic and atomized society. Truly humane values – love, solidarity, etc. – are devalued by capitalism. At present the New Right is trying to overcome this contradiction by emphasizing traditional values like the family and patriotism, but the left can respond more effectively by showing how social and moral disintegration are rooted in late capitalism.

The central contradiction of contemporary capitalism however is that it is increasingly undemocratic. Economic and political power are concentrated and centralized; the average citizen plays no role in running the giant corporations. In the political sphere, it is only centralized organizations, like business associations and trade lobbies, that play major roles in the selection of our political leaders. And of course it is the control of the media by these organizations and the bourgeoisie that determines what political options and messages are presented to voters. Moreover, Watergate and Contragate show the darker sides of 'imperial' presidencies and a general contempt for constitutional procedures.

It is the 'death of democracy' that the left can use as a political banner in the United States to challenge the hold of the bourgeoisie. In this struggle, the left can reclaim the US past, including historic milestones like the Declaration of Independence. It can appeal to the country's progressive political tradition which includes anti-war movements as well as political leaders like Tom Paine, Abraham Lincoln, Eugene Debs, Robert La Follette, and Martin Luther King Jr.

Another major challenge for the left in the United States is to reclaim patriotism from the right. In the twentieth century, the US ruling classes have made patriotism virtually synonymous with anti-communism, anti-Sovietism, and now anti-terrorism. To support any of these causes is to be fundamentally 'anti-American'.

The left needs to reassert the revolutionary values of 1776 and 1860. Sectors of the third force today are far more supportive than the bourgeoisie of the national and democratic values that this nation was founded on. It is corporate capital and the national security state that are destroying basic values and denying foreign countries right to self-determination, the very right on which the USA was founded when it rebelled against England in 1776.

4

The Internationalization of Struggle in the Americas

The Americas, more than any other part of the world, possess the social raw material for a new revolutionary vision. The countries in the Western Hemisphere contain the most advanced capitalist society – the United States – and the most developed third world societies – Argentina, Brazil and Mexico. Taken together, the Americas constitute the most powerful and productive area in the world. These societies can still be appropriately described as the 'New World'. They have an enormous creative and dynamic energy that is manifested in their popular cultures, their literature and their arts. Ethnically and racially, they are still 'melting pots' bringing together an incredible array of peoples from Africa, Europe and Asia as well as indigenous cultures.

Increasingly, the destinies of the societies of the Americas are interlinked. The emergence of the fourth force is rooted in this reality. This trend began with the Cuban revolution in 1959 which involved a whole new generation of internationalists. After seizing power the revolutionaries in Cuba demonstrated an unprecedented internationalism, supporting revolutionary movements throughout Latin America. Simultaneously, the first signs of reciprocal international support began to appear, as evinced by the Fair Play for Cuba Committee, a US organization which sought to oppose the interventionist policies of the US government.[1] The Vietnam War had a further critical impact on the development of solidarity and the rise of the fourth force in the Americas.

Wherever one went in the late 1960s, be it the United States, Chile, Venezuela, or Peru, one would find organizations that were supporting the Vietnamese. These movements laid the basis for the flowering of solidarity movements around Latin American revolutionary struggles in the 1970s.[2]

Just how far the internationalization of revolutionary struggle in the Americas has advanced was demonstrated by the support for the Nicaraguan revolution in 1979. This was a poor, backward society that was virtually ignored by the rest of the world. But once the Sandinista struggle against the Somoza regime began to reach crisis proportions, an array of international actors were drawn into the conflict. The United States, in an effort to maintain its historic control over Nicaragua, first tried to defuse the crisis by getting Somoza to carry out limited reforms; when this failed, the Carter administration began to conspire with the local opposition bourgeoisie to find a new alternative. At the same time, the progressive forces in the Americas mobilized around the FSLN to help overthrow the Somoza regime. Chileans, Argentines, Hondurans and many others participated directly in the revolutionary struggle while arms came from sympathetic governments and supporters in Panama, Costa Rica, Colombia and Cuba. In the United States, a solidarity movement was built in 1978 and 1979 that made it virtually impossible for the Carter administration to intervene directly to block the Sandinistas from taking power.

The experiences of the revolutionary movements of the 1960s and 1970s were also brought to fruit in Nicaragua. The Sandinista leadership itself was the product of the revolutionary ferment of these earlier periods. Over 200 members of the Sandinista Front had been present as observers or participants in revolutionary struggles in Chile, Argentina, Guatemala and other parts of Latin America and the Caribbean. There was even an intercontinental component with some of the Frente members having been in Angola, the Middle East and Vietnam.

In sum, the success of the Sandinista revolution owed almost as much to the mobilization of international forces and pressures against the Somoza regime as it did to the internal upheaval within Nicaragua. In many ways, the Sandinista revolution was a synthesis of the rich revolutionary ferment that had swept the Americas from 1959. Perhaps even more importantly, the Nicaraguan revolution has served as an inspiration and a 'political laboratory' for tens of thousands of people who have come to Nicaragua to work and to experience first hand the revolutionary process. Hondurans, Mexicans, Dominicans, Haitians, Peruvians, Puerto Ricans, and many others have come to Nicaragua to contribute and to learn. The largest contingent of internationalists has come from the United States. It is estimated that over 100,000 Americans have visited Nicaragua since 1979, coming to spend a few weeks or months to join in work brigades, or simply to experience the uniqueness and importance of the Nicaraguan revolution. And hundreds, if not thousands, have stayed for extended periods to contribute their skills and talents. The experiences accumulated by the internationalists have been brought home throughout the Americas, accelerating the process of internationalism.

The Internationalization of Class Conflict

The Nicaraguan revolution expressed what is an increasingly important phenomenon in the late-twentieth century: the internationalization of class conflict. As the societies of the Americas become more and more interlinked, there is a tendency for class struggles to spill over national boundaries and to have regional and international repercussions. The national liberation movements are the clearest embodiment of this dialectic. The Cuban Revolution marked the turning point where class struggles began to have international ramifications throughout the Americas. Today in Chile, Peru, Colombia, El Salvador and Guatemala revolutionary movements continue this process. Their leadership is internationalist in vision and they receive political and material aid from peoples beyond their borders. And the advance of any single movement encourages other liberation movements, thereby accelerating the process of class conflict on a regional and international basis.

But the internationalization of class conflict is broader than the revolutionary movements. Conflicts and disputes between non-revolutionary states and the United States are the products of class tensions and social pressures brought to bear by the masses on their respective governments. These popular pressures, combined with local bourgeois discontent, explain why the largest countries in Latin America –

Argentina, Brazil and Mexico – have taken increasingly divergent stands from those of the United States. The debt crisis, the Malvinas conflict, the Contradora process, and the opposing stands often taken around critical issues in the Organization of the American States (OAS) reflect the growing contradictions between the national interests of the United States and the countries of Latin America and the Caribbean. The growing complexity of the Latin American economies, the increasingly important role of the national bourgeoisies, and the global economic crisis that has led the United States to throw up protectionist barriers and to extract more surplus from Latin America – all directly affect the local ruling classes and stimulate a more independent self-interest.

But it would be a mistake to believe that the growing inter-hemispheric tensions are mainly rooted in conflicts between Washington and the national bourgeoisies. To a large extent the governments of Latin America are compelled to stand up to US imperialism by popular pressures from below. Food riots in the Dominican Republic and Brazil, and national strikes against austerity programs in Bolivia, Argentina, Equador and Peru, have forced the governments of these countries to take tougher stands against the international bankers and to be more demanding in their commercial and economic relations with the United States.

The Ties That Bind

The United States is now profoundly affected by the social forces at work south of its borders, while the societies of the Latin and Caribbean countries are also continually affected by what happens in the United States. National boundaries have been eroded by powerful economic, social and political forces, while immigration ties together the countries of the Americas as never before. In the United States the peoples of Latin and Caribbean origin are assuming increasing importance, particularly in the Sunbelt and New York. They are now on the verge of passing the Black population as the largest third world sector and they will become even more important as the century advances.

Burgeoning immigration is an index of the degree to which US transnational banks and corporations are breaking down national barriers and creating new economic interdependencies. Today it is not only the Latin American economies that are dependent; the United States also finds that its economy is affected by developments in the Caribbean and Latin America. Moreover, the explosion of US financial investments in Latin America during the past decade has linked the health and survival of the domestic banking system to the ability of the largest Latin American countries to repay their debts, while the recent debt-produced recession in Latin America has cost tens of thousands of US manufacturing jobs.

Equally significant, political developments in the United States, Latin America and the Caribbean are increasingly interlinked. The general crisis of the US empire has dramatic repercussions for the third world societies that are geographically closest to the United States. It is no accident that the very regions where the modern American empire first consolidated itself – in the Caribbean and Central America as well as in parts of South America and the Philippines – are now the scenes of upheaval and conflict. These societies more than any other in the world bear the scars of US domination. Their economic, political and social orders have been shaped by imperatives emanating from the United States, and accordingly, the decline of US hegemony and the global crisis of capitalism means that the societies most closely bound to the United States are the most profoundly affected.

Simultaneously, the decline of the American empire has political repercussions within the United States. As Contragate has demonstrated: now more than ever the imperial crisis is being internalized. Latin American issues once captured US headlines only when there was a military coup, a 'Communist threat' in the hemisphere, or when US gunboats or marines intervened. Now on any given day one is more likely than not to find a major news story on issues like the Latin American debt crisis, the Contra war against Nicaragua, or the political situation in Mexico, Argentina or Brazil. And at the highest levels, the executive branch as well as the Congress and an array of elite think tanks are devoting ever increasing attention to developments in the Caribbean and Latin America.

Both right wing and progressive forces in the United States see the conflict in Central America as an integral part of their political program. The Reagan administration and its New Right ideologues look to the evangelical churches, rightwing corporate leaders, retired military officials and 'soldiers of fortune' to further its program in Central America and the Caribbean. The anti-interventionist movement on the other hand finds its ranks expanding with support from the Catholic and mainline Protestant churches, and research and publication centers that adopt a critical perspective towards the US role.

National Liberation and the New Bolivarism

The internationalization of class conflict in Latin America has nurtured the resurgence of 'Bolivarism', a historic movement going back to Latin American independence that seeks to unify the countries of the Southern hemisphere against outside interests.[3] This movement acquired particular momentum during the Malvinas War in 1982. The decision of Washington to side with Great Britain in the conflict demonstrated to even the rightwing governments of Latin America that the dominant capitalist countries will always maintain a united front against challenges from the third world. During the war most of the countries of Latin America, regardless of their political orientation, rallied behind Argentina. Only Chile which has a longstanding border dispute with Argentina, and a few US and British client states, particularly in the Caribbean, supported Great Britain.

Behind this shift in the political alignment of the hemisphere is the reality that the national liberation movements have compelled the governments of Latin America and the Caribbean to take non-interventionist and even anti-imperialist stands. The convergence of liberation movements and Bolivarism is perhaps most evident in the Contadora process in Central America, in which the largest nations of Latin America (representing over 80% of its population) have taken a stand against US intervention that objectively aids the revolutionary movements in Central America. For the first time in modern history a group of non-revolutionary governments have taken the initiative in trying to find a 'Latin American' solution to a crisis in which the United States is intent on imposing a counterrevolution. Continual US efforts to sabotage and undermine the Contadora process make it difficult for the participant countries to negotiate an end to the Central American conflict, but the very fact that a group of Latin American countries has tried to chart a new course is one more indication of the growing divergence between Latin American and US state interests.

Beyond the East-West and North-South Conflicts

Bolivarism and the general internationalization of class conflict have opened up the Americas to other international actors, particularly Western Europe and the Socialist bloc. In the effort to find alternatives to US domination, many Latin American and Caribbean countries of the region look to other powers for assistance. Western Europe has offered limited but at times crucial help. For example French diplomatic support for the FMLN in El Salvador was important in the early 1980s. But continual pressure from the United States along with rejection of Social Democratic models by the Salvadoran and Nicaraguan revolutionary movements has led most Western European governments to pull back from their independent stands in Central America and to endorse US policies to some extent.

Help provided by the Socialist bloc countries, on the other hand, has tended to increase in a fairly steady and consistent manner. There is no doubt that Soviet aid, first for Cuba, and then for Nicaragua, has enabled these revolutions to survive and to challenge basic us interests in the hemisphere. During the past decade the Soviet Union has given more financial and military aid to the national liberation movements than previously. In the 1960s and early 1970s the Soviet Union remained tied to the political positions staked out by the Communist parties of Latin America. These parties were opposed to armed struggle and embraced reformist and electoral political strategies. Serious divisions existed between Cuba and the Soviet Union over support for the guerrilla movements in Latin America, divisions that even led to Soviet cutbacks in economic assistance to Cuba. In the early 1970s Soviet interest in détente with the United States reinforced its tendency to eschew involvement in third world struggles.

Then in the mid 1970s the Soviet position began to shift. First the overthrow of the elected socialist government of Salvador Allende in Chile in 1973, and then Cuba's decision to send troops to Angola in 1974 to fight against the South

Africans helped goad the Soviet Union into becoming more supportive of national liberation movements. A crisis within the Latin American Communist parties, and the decision of the Communist parties in El Salvador and Chile to include armed struggle in their programs also facilitated a shift in Soviet attitudes. By the time of the ousting of Somoza, the Soviet Union was demonstrating a much more flexible and supportive position towards national liberation movements.

However, the Soviet role in supporting national liberation movements in the hemisphere – whether or not a persistent trend – does not mean that Latin America and the Caribbean should now be seen simply as arenas for the East-West conflict. Each new conflict in the Americas results in an ever growing number of regional and extra-regional actors. This is an inevitable historic tendency that will accelerate in the coming years.

At the same time it is inappropriate to try to place hemispheric conflicts in the North-South framework. One cannot view these conflicts as simply pitting the rich and the poor nations of the Americas against each other. Fundamentally these are conflicts in which the US ruling class is ever more closely aligned with the local elites in an effort to crush the popular forces. Simultaneously, US society is also divided, with certain sectors opposing imperialist policies and providing important assistance to liberation movements like those in Nicaragua and El Salvador. What we are seeing in the Americas in the 1980s is an advanced stage of struggle that is breaking down national boundaries.

Solidarity and the Politics of Revolution

To understand how this conflict affects the United States, it is necessary to consider the divisions that exist over imperialist policies and how they shape the solidarity movement and the emerging 'fourth force'. In recent years there has been a tendency by many analysts to develop a 'sociology of imperialism'. They examine the economic and military instruments of intervention and analyze the distinct sectors of the ruling class in an effort to discover the determinants of interventionism. This work has been useful in educating many people, particularly in the United States, about the nature of imperialism. But what many of these studies fail to recognize is that US imperialism is limited – even contained at times – by other factors, particularly by the development of revolutionary and popular movements in the third world, and by the development of anti-imperialist and non-intervention movements in the United States.

Within US society, foreign interventions have produced two contradictory reactions. On the one hand, intervention has stimulated the growth of domestic movements that oppose Washington's counterrevolutionary policies. First the Vietnam war, and then subsequent interventions – ranging from the CIA backed coup in Chile in 1973 to the current US military buildup in Central America – have sparked major opposition movements. However, the very growth of the anti-intervention movements combined with the erosion of US power abroad have fomented the development of an opposing tendency – a right wing movement that demands the ardent defense of imperial interests against all third world radical movements.

This polarization over foreign policy issues reflects the fundamental crisis of the US empire. Because the informal empire that was forged in the early twentieth century is an integral part of the US system, it is logical that its disintegration would inevitably have profound reverberations within the United States. As the conflicts in El Salvador and Nicaragua demonstrate, the loss or threatened loss of small countries that have historically been in the US sphere of influence spark domestic debates that divide opinion into distinct political camps.

The development of this debate is related to the impact the crisis of the US empire has on different social sectors. The dominant strata of US society are driven to defend hemispheric hegemony because they have a material interest in doing so. The corporate elites, the beneficiaries of the military-industrial complex, and the state managers who run the foreign policy apparatus – these groups all have a definite stake in preserving US domination and preventing third world societies from breaking out of the system.

Aligned with the military and corporate interests are the foreign policy managers who jockey for positions of power and reap promotions and material benefits by 'protecting US interest' abroad. And grouped around these state managers are many think tanks, foreign policy associations and lobbies that are funded by private business groups or by lucrative government contracts. They use their power and influence to reinforce the belief that US society as a whole will be undermined if revolutionary movements in the third world are not contained or defeated.

The Domestic Adversaries of Empire

There are broad sectors of US society — minorities, the white working class, most of the middle class, many women, and even certain business sectors — that do not have such a direct stake in US hegemony. Some of these groups did benefit from US expansion in the past, particularly in the early cold war period when US power reached its apogee. The growth of export markets in the developed and underdeveloped worlds, the inflow of profits from US corporate expansion abroad, and the creation of a military-industrial complex — these and other varieties of 'military Keynesianism' created jobs, generated income, and in general contributed to the growing prosperity of US society.

However, the Vietnam war combined with the erosion of the US global economic position in the late 1960s and early 1970s reduced the rewards of empire that accrued to the lower strata of US society. No real cost-benefit sheet can be drawn up on who gains or loses from US imperialism at any given moment, but one can perceive that as challenges arose to US prerogatives abroad — challenges from third world revolutionary movements, from Western European and Japanese economic competitors, and even from newly industrializing third world countries — fewer benefits trickled down to the general populace. Moreover as the challenges to US domination mounted, the costs of defending the empire were borne disproportionately by the lower social sectors. The Vietnam war demonstrated that Blacks and Latinos along with white working class youth would pay inordinately in blood and wasted lives to preserve informal empire.

Today Reaganomics is a clear declaration of who will pay the price necessary to prop up the US empire in its waning years. From 1981 to 1985 the military-industrial complex consumed an ever expanding percentage of the national wealth while fundamental social programs (medical care, educational programs, unemployment benefits, housing facilities, etc.) were curtailed or eliminated. This was not paid for, of course, by the wealthy or the corporations, whose tax rates dramatically decreased, but by the middle and lower strata.

The Emerging Alternative

During the past quarter century the anti-interventionist movements have become a significant force in domestic politics, and the core of the fourth force in the United States. Allied with or part of this force are the anti-nuclear movements; the increasingly militant protests against US support for apartheid; the solidarity organizations that mobilize public sympathy in the United States for revolutionary movements in countries like the Philippines, El Salvador, Nicaragua, and Chile; the growing number of local trade union committees that challenge the cold war positions of their national trade union leadership; the many Catholic, Jewish, and mainline Protestant churches who support basic human rights and the principles of self-determination. These are some of the domestic social and political forces that are working to build, piece-by-piece, a new vision of a non-interventionist foreign policy.

At the same time small research and lobbying organizations are generating new policy perspectives based on non-intervention, an end to US militarism, and respect for the principle of self-determination. Some of these organizations are based in Washington, while others are scattered around the United States. They engage in varied activities ranging from the publication of special reports, magazines and books to organizing public forums and the production of posters and audio-visual materials. Although virtually all are under-staffed and operate on shoestring budgets, they are having a broad impact, partly through the Rainbow Coalition, and are providing the only effective critiques of the interventionist policies of the Reagan administration and the New Right.

Polarization over Central America

It was perhaps inevitable that the Reagan foreign policy, tied as it is to Reaganomics and the new inequality, would precipitate a backlash from the social sectors that had nothing to gain from interventionist policies.

The widening social cleavage over US foreign policy is most clearly manifested in the domestic struggle over intervention in Central America and the Caribbean, which today, as never before, is dividing the body politic between right wing and progressive positions.

From the beginning the Reagan administration moved to mobilize corporate support for its hemispheric strategy. The Caribbean Central American Action (C/CAA) organization, a little known but influential group of business leaders from many of the country's leading corporations, began to work closely with the administration in 1981 to encourage the broader business community to invest in the Caribbean Basin and to publicly support Reagan's counterrevolutionary policies.[4] Subsequently, right-wing business groups in the United States were mobilized to back the Reagan administration's efforts to topple the Sandinista government. When in 1984 Congress attempted to restrict the CIA's ability to fund and direct the Contras, 'free enterprise', under the direction of Oliver North, stepped in to provide assistance. Reagan backers J. Peter Grace and Adolph Coors raised millions of dollars in Contra aid from business and corporate donors. Right-wing evangelical churches also raised millions which was given, in addition to the Contras, to like-minded religious groups in Guatemala and El Salvador. At the same time mercenaries were recruited by groups linked to the *Soldier of Fortune* magazine to advise the Contras and even to fight with them in Nicaragua. This 'privatization' of the war, and the appeal to specific right-wing groups to become directly involved in counterrevolutionary warfare, represents an unprecedented development in US history.

Simultaneously, the forces opposed to US intervention have also deepened their roots, giving the anti-war movement a much broader social base today than it had during the Vietnam war. Campuses are perhaps less prominent, but that lack is more than compensated for by the involvement of the religious community. Mainline Protestant churches, Catholic bishops, liberation theologists, religious orders and local church congregations have all realized that fundamental moral principles are being violated by the Reagan Doctrine. Moreover, through the Sanctuary movement, church leaders are taking a stand on behalf of Salvadoran and Central

American refugees in the United States. The religious community also plays a key role in the Pledge of Resistance network, whose 100,000 signers have committed themselves to civil disobedience if the United States intervenes more directly in Central America.

The maturation of the solidarity organizations and their efforts to reach out to new social sectors have been of critical importance in building opposition to interventionist policies. Few of these groups talk in the rhetorical and alienating language that was often heard during the 1960s; instead they concentrate on presenting their messages in a rhetoric and style that are rooted in basic American values and beliefs, such as democracy, freedom and the right to self-determination.

Today, the anti-intervention movement is a major force that is able to challenge the influence of the well-heeled and well-financed right wing. This is why President Reagan and other New Right figures constantly complain that they cannot get their interventionist message across to the American people and decry the 'disinformation campaigns' of opposition forces. Public opinion polls indicate the vast majority of the American people do not believe that US troops should be in Central America, nor do they think that we should prop up right wing authoritarian regimes, even if they are 'guardians against communism'.[5]

Reagan's policies have also polarized politics in Latin America. Throughout the Americas, the popular classes are increasingly aware that the Sandinista revolution is fighting to defend a common principle of sovereignty. The solidarity movements with Nicaragua, extending from Brazil and Uruguay to Argentina, Mexico, Cuba and Canada, are much more militant and developed than any comparable movements in the past. They include not only the traditional leftist political parties and the trade unions, but also many third force sectors, such as academics, women's organizations, barrio residents, religious leaders, etc. Increasingly they feel that the struggles of other peoples, like those of Nicaragua, are their own, and they are nourished by a Bolivarian and Latin Americanist perspective. Perhaps even more importantly, these sectors and organizations are conscious of the difference between the imperialist interests of the US ruling classes and those of the US people. Meetings, discussions, exchange programs, etc. between US, Caribbean and Latin

American peoples now occur on a regular basis. Over the past decade, solidarity organizations, universities, and even towns and cities have set up special programs and exchanges that tie together people at the grassroots levels in the United States and Central America.[6]

The emergence and growth of the anti-imperialist movement is no accident nor is it a transitory phenomenon. Temporary setbacks, such as the decision of Congress in 1986 to renew military aid to the Contras, should not be viewed as decisive. They are part of the ebb and flow that will inevitably occur in the battle ahead. As the crisis of imperialism deepens in the late twentieth century, the anti-intervention movement, or the fourth force, will grow in complexity and play an increasingly important role in providing support for third world revolutions. Perhaps, even more importantly, anti-imperialism will have a critical impact on the US political system and become a major force in challenging the established party-political order. The extent and depth of this movement are new phenomena in the development of imperialist societies. It is the domestic antithesis of imperialism, and it is no accident that the most developed fourth force exists in the bowels of the leading imperialist power, the United States.

5

The Challenge of the 1990s

There is a war raging in the Americas. It is a war between US-led mercenaries and a revolutionary army in Nicaragua. It is a war between US-backed armies and guerrilla forces in Colombia, El Salvador and Guatemala. It is also a war fought by striking workers and urban demonstrators against repressive police and military forces in the Dominican Republic, Uruguay, Brazil, Chile and Haiti. The Americas are in the throes of a crisis rooted in the decline of the American empire. The retreat of the military regimes in Brazil, Argentina, Uruguay and Peru, the downfall of Duvalier in Haiti, the mass protests against IMF-imposed austerity programs in the Dominican Republic, Brazil and Bolivia, and the political instability of governments in Ecuador, Jamaica and Panama are all signs that the popular classes are in motion, that they are questioning the status quo and searching for new alternatives.

A fundamental difference exists between the situation we face today in the wake of the Nicaraguan revolution, and the one we faced after the Cuban revolution. In the 1960s and for most of the 1970s, capitalism was an extremely dynamic force in Latin America. It profoundly altered much of the hemisphere, developing new arenas of capital accumulation in the countryside and the cities. A new productive bourgeoisie emerged, based in industry and agriculture. The middle class expanded rapidly and the peasantry swarmed to the cities in search of work.

But the revolutionizing dynamic of capitalism is no longer ascendant. The global economic crisis has ended the expansive period. If any sector of the bourgeoisie is now expanding in Latin America, it is the most speculative sector, the sector linked to commerce, banking, black market activities and even drug trafficking. Chile in the 1970s, with its 'Chicago Boys', was the laboratory for testing this model. There a whole new economic sector emerged based on importation and financial speculation while the productive bourgeoisie was largely decimated.

The debt crisis which developed in the early 1980s has drawn most Latin American countries deeper into the embrace of international finance capital. Under the aegis of the International Monetary Fund, austerity programs and free market measures have been imposed, breaking down national barriers to foreign capital. To prevent the collapse of the international financial system, the United States has moved in to support the more favoured regimes with special loans from the Federal Reserve Bank, from the Agency for International Development (AID) and from a variety of institutions under the auspices of the so-called 'Baker Plan'. These policies are designed to tie a select group of countries of the third world even closer to the United States, while privatizing their state sectors and trading part of their debt for new, US-owned equity.

In Central America, the banana republics have now been replaced by the 'AID republics'. These small countries are each subsidized annually to the tune of hundreds of millions of dollars because they have a strategic political role to play in Reagan's war against the Nicaraguan revolution. The Central American military and the local elites are placed on the US dole while their countries are ravaged by war and by the drop in the global prices of raw materials. This inflow of funds further corrupts the already venal military, and state bureaucracies, as well as fueling a speculative petty mercantile perspective.

It's paradoxical that the militaries and the local elites in Central America owe their new-found prosperity entirely to the Nicaraguan revolution. If the Sandinistas had not come to power, they would be languishing in the economic and political backwaters of Latin America, receiving only token assistance from the United States. The continued survival of the Sandinista government is, ironically, in the interests of these elites since it guarantees that they can remain on the Washington payroll in the name of fighting 'communism and totalitarianism'.

In South America, the current economic crisis has had a somewhat different impact. Many sectors of the bourgeoisie, which had benefitted from collaboration with US imperialism for years, are now for the first time suffering at its hands. The United States and the IMF are hitting at the national bourgeoisies, restricting domestic markets with austerity programs, reducing investment flows to the state sectors, and dismantling protections against US imports. These bourgeoisies face stepped up competition from foreign products while their own products are subject to increasing restrictions in the US market. Within specific limits, this inclines them to support 'anti-imperialist' stances, and this is one reason why Nicaragua enjoys support even among some bourgeois governments in Latin America.

To understand the economic crisis and some of its political ramifications, it is useful to categorize the distinct types of economies that prevail in Latin America and the Caribbean.

First there are the mono-producer or agro-export economies which are in a state of paralysis. These economies are dependent on one crop or mineral, or on the export of raw materials in general. They are victims of unequal exchange in the international markets, a situation which is exacerbated today by the unprecedented depression of the prices of most raw materials. Some of these countries are formally democratic, but virtually all of them have weak civilian institutions. It is in these societies where the crisis and the revolutionary potential is the greatest. This category includes most of the Central American republics, Bolivia, the Dominican Republic, Haiti, Jamaica, and other Caribbean countries.

Secondly there are the economies at an intermediate stage of development, mainly located on the Pacific coast of South America. These countries have developed significant industrial structures, but they are still heavily dependent on primary exports. Peru, Ecuador, Colombia, Chile and Mexico belong in this category. In these societies the crisis is also profound: the local bourgeoisies and militaries are still intact and have by no means played out their options, but social forces are in motion, especially in Peru and Chile.

Finally there are the countries with the most diverse and developed capitalist infrastructure in Latin America – Brazil,

Argentina and Venezuela. Here the economic crisis does take its toll, but the bourgeoisies display a high degree of resilience. In Brazil a section of the economic elite has openly opposed the IMF-imposed recession and temporarily was able to stimulate a new cycle of growth. These societies are most similar to societies of the first world. Their immediate revolutionary potential is perhaps not as great as in other countries in Latin America, but they will play decisive roles in the reshaping of socio-economic structures in the hemisphere.

Economic Crisis and Revolution

What does the economic situation portend for the future of the revolutionary movements? Traditionally Marxists have portrayed economic crises as an essential ingredient for precipitating a revolutionary situation. In reality, history demonstrates that economic crises play only a limited role in creating revolutionary opportunities. During capitalism's greatest economic crisis, the depression of the 1930s, not a single socialist revolution occurred. Neither the Cuban nor the Nicaraguan revolutions were the products of economic crises or depressions. Indeed, the economies of both countries were in a state of expansion until the final stages of the revolutionary struggle.

If history has any lessons to teach us it is that there are two broad preconditions for a political revolution: 1) the existence of major conflicts within or between the ruling classes, and 2) the existence of a dynamic popular movement with a revolutionary program. A capitalist society will never fall of its own weight. During the great depression, the first condition actually existed in that there were both inter- and intra-bourgeois conflicts. But the popular classes were not strong enough to prevent the ruling classes in the Western countries from consolidating around one of two options: – Keynesian reformism or fascism. It was only the direct conflict between these two blocs in the Second World War that opened the way for the expansion of socialism in the postwar period.

Today serious conflicts among ruling classes are leading to fissures in the system of domination. But this crisis in the ruling bloc will lead nowhere if the popular movements and the revolutionary forces do not act. US imperialism under

Ronald Reagan has already set in motion a two-pronged offensive for reconsolidating its rule in the Americas. It involves: 1) an offensive against US working people, including a rollback in real wages and the slashing of social programs, and 2) the use of military force in Latin America and the Caribbean, and the imposition of tough economic measures that benefit US multinational interests. The bottom line for the US bourgeoisie is to increase the economic surplus so that it can rebuild its economic base and deal with its accumulation crisis. The success or failure of this program hinges on what the popular classes and the revolutionary movements do in Latin America, the Caribbean and the United States. Left to its own devices, the US ruling class will very likely succeed. Only strong opposition from the lower classes and a redynamized left can stop it. The struggle will not be easy. The days when Fidel Castro and a band of a dozen men were able to implant themselves in the Sierra Maestra and carry out a political revolution in the short span of two years are probably not destined to happen again.

Today the struggles will be longer and more difficult. Most societies in Latin America and the Caribbean are much more complex, and imperialism has learned well the lessons of history. The US New Right is determined to prevent another Cuba or Nicaragua, and as we have seen in the Philippines and in Haiti, the United States will even help precipitate the fall of dictators that it helped put in power, hoping to deprive the revolutionary of an anti-dictatorial banner.

The Deepening Conflict in Civil Society

It is necessary to remain one step ahead of the rightwing offensive. In the past revolutionary movements have focused on the political sphere, on electoral and parliamentary struggles, and on guerrilla and military struggles, especially under repressive regimes. These struggles will continue to be important in the future, but their success will depend on what happens in civil society. It is only there that we can begin to forge new alternatives, to build new values, to change the conceptions of daily life and of social relations. In sum it is in civil society where we develop a new conception of the world, a dynamic and living alternative to the established bourgeois order.

The conflict in civil society is already well advanced. In Argentina and Guatemala, organizations of the mothers of the disappeared, by demanding justice for their missing sons and daughters, are challenging and undermining the most powerful institution of all in Latin America, the local militaries. In Peru, the struggle in civil society is occurring on many fronts: in the *pueblos jovenes*, or barrios, where political and economic education programs are taking place; in the large demonstrations and strikes called by the trade unions and left political parties; and also in the participation of the United Left parties in local and national elections where issues of socialism and national liberation are debated and discussed.

In Brazil, the struggle in civil society is being conducted within the Catholic Church, the bastion of the old order; in the mobilizations of the trade unions; and in the conflicts over how to shape the country's political system in the aftermath of military rule. In Jamaica, the announced showcase for Reaganomics in the third world, the battle in civil society is carried out in the violence that erupts with ever increasing frequency in the streets of Kingston, and in the increasing delegitimization of the political system in general. And in Honduras, the US military presence is slowly but surely undermining the old structures of civil society, as peasant and women's organizations, local newspapers, and even members of the local congress protest the sellout of the country.

Culture is another critical front in this struggle. Over the years the cultural left has been putting forth values and ideas that influence broad sectors of society. The social protest novel started with Asturias in the 1950s, but since then many authors have taken up its themes, including Gabriel Garcia Márquez, Carpentier, Julio Cortazar, Carlos Fuentes, Eduardo Galeano, Isabel Allende, and many others. Poetry also has seen a renaissance on the left, including Pablo Neruda, Rocque Dalton and Ernesto Cardenal. It is no exaggeration to say that poets and novelists in Latin America have played a much more important role than social scientists in raising the political consciousness of the masses against authoritarian regimes and imperialism.

The revolutionary songs of Carlos Pueblo and Silvio Rodriguez in Cuba, the popular music of Allende's Chile, and the wave of protest music – Cancion Nueva – that surged through the Americas including the United States in the 1960s have had a dramatic impact on mass culture. Film has also become a means for putting forth a progressive, and even revolutionary perspective, not only in countries like Brazil, and Argentina, but also in the United States where today even Hollywood is willing to release progressive films like *Missing*, *Under Fire*, and *Latino*.

Theory, Political Strategy and Civil Society

One major weakness of the current struggles in civil society is that they are often unrelated and uncoordinated. These struggles erupt in particular areas, and their effect is often minimized because only a limited awareness exists of what they signify for the evolution of society as a whole. If the struggles in civil society are to reach a new level of sophistication and development, it is important to understand how they can relate to a revolutionary process.

Bourgeois hegemony is not based simply on its control of political institutions. Indeed its capacity to maintain democratic institutions and to weather severe economic crisis is due to the permeation of bourgeois values and ideas throughout civil society. This is why we assign such importance to the third force, particularly the petty bourgeoisie and the middle class who hold strategic positions in the cultural and ideological centers of capitalism, i.e. in the media, in the schools and universities, and in the socio-political structures that operate at the community level. These social sectors are the 'opinion molders' and 'organic intellectuals' of contemporary society, and a shift in their perspective has wide ideological repercussions.

The rise of the so-called 'Peoples' Republic of Berkeley' in California demonstrates how critical it is for changes to occur in the values and ideology of civil society before advances can be made in the political arena. In the 1960s, Berkeley became a center of intellectual and social activism. The Free Speech Movement, the Vietnam Day Committee, the draft resistance, the emergence of alternative newspapers, the intense discussions of art, culture and politics, the development of alternative life styles, and the rise of Black power and third world consciousness – all contributed to transforming traditional bourgeois values in Berkeley and the surrounding metropolitan area.

Eventually the social movements, the churches, the schools and even the trade unions and working class were affected by these new ideas. When in the mid-1970s, radicalized white and middle class groups joined with Black and third world organizations in a political alliance over issues of rent control, housing, police repression and community services, the basis was laid for the election of a socialist mayor and a progressive majority to the Berkeley city council. Today the left is so well entrenched that the New Right has no visible presence and it is the Democratic liberals who are trying to pose a viable alternative to the city's social democratic leadership.

The Rainbow Coalition presents a similar political alternative at a national level. At the present this popular insurgency remains focused on Jessie Jackson's crusade to turn the Democratic party leftward. But unlike the purely electoralist left, the Rainbow does not view its future as inextricably tied to that of the Democratic party. Its basic objective is not to win party nominations, but to advance a set of political principles and policies that are fundamentally radical in the context of current US politics. Its commitment to civil rights and civil liberties for Blacks, Latins, women and gays, its opposition to federal cutbacks for domestic programs and its advocacy of decent living standards for the poor, its support for dramatic arms reductions and a nuclear weapons freeze, and its steadfast opposition to US intervention abroad – have become principles and policies over which the Coalition will not negotiate.

Simultaneously, the Coalition has an 'inside-outside' political strategy. It does work inside the Democratic party, but it also works outside the party in all levels of society to advance its own political program. The people it mobilizes are mobilized around a set of issues, not around the Democratic party. The idea is to build an independent power bloc, one that can be used to advance a progressive political and social agenda, not to enhance the electoral clout of the Democratic party.

As some leaders of the Rainbow Coalition themselves recognize, there are certain dangers in this political strategy. The coalition could get too caught up in pursuing an electoral strategy within the Democratic party, or at the other extreme, it could form a separate party and fall by the wayside like so many other third parties in US history. The key to its future depends on whether or not it can become a new 'social force' in the United States, whether it can expand its social base while creating a new ideological perspective that poses a popular alternative to the social, economic and political inequalities that are tacitly integral to both the Republican and Democratic party platforms. This approach may not lead to any immediate political victories, but it could dynamize the social movements and the progressive political causes, placing their issues and concerns on the national political agenda.

The Multi-Front Insurrection

We need to develop a revolutionary perspective that links the many different fronts of struggle in Latin America, the Caribbean and the United States. Today, we need to be insurrectional, not just in the final moment of the political struggle, but in our ideas, in our daily lives, in the organizations in which we participate, and in our dreams for a new world. Nor can we limit our hopes and our demands to the economic sphere: to do so is to fall into the trap of capitalism, since in that terrain it has the decisive advantage.

We have to seize the ideological initiative from the New Right, end our historic isolation, and carry on the battle throughout civil society. Because of the complex nature of capitalist societies and the determination of imperialism to prop up the old order, this battle will be long and arduous. It is no accident that the intense struggles in Chile, in El Salvador, in Colombia and in the Philippines have been going on for years. Victories will come, but they will be hard fought and hard won. Our revolutionary optimism must be tempered by calculation and realism, and our urgency to undertake each struggle should be balanced by a certain calm and tranquility going into each battle.

In this unfolding struggle it is important for the political parties on the left to put aside their sectarian differences and to begin working together. This was the key to the Sandinista triumph. In most countries today no single party has the potential to be the vanguard. To quote Tom Paine, an early 'internationalista', 'we must must all hang together or we will all hang separately'. Political fronts, coalitions and unified blocs of parties are the only options. It is imperative to begin coordinating our work so there can be a political division of labor.

Political practice has advanced significantly in recent years. One can even detect signs that dogmatism and sectarianism are giving way to collective and creative fraternalism in many parts of the Americas. Today many different strategies that were once in conflict are being merged. The struggle in legal political institutions is combined with clandestine struggle, while armed struggle is combined with work among the masses. The dramatic shift in the political strategy of the Communist party in Chile, the unification of the Salvadoran parties in the FMLN, and the rise of the Coordinadora in Colombia, are all important examples of how different political perspectives and strategies are being united in common political fronts to foment an ever deepening revolutionary process.

It is also necessary for revolutionary formations to expand their international horizons and to learn from other experiences. Revolutions will spill over the borders of the Americas in the years to come. It has already happened, even in the United States where civil society has been profoundly affected by imperial wars. Blacks and Latinos as well as whites will learn lessons from their brothers and sisters to the south. It will become gradually recognized that socialism can emerge in the small countries to the south without threatening the integrity of the US nation; many sectors of US society that were once manipulated by a fear of 'Soviet communism' are today opening to new political perspectives that arise out of the social and revolutionary movements in Latin America and the Caribbean.

The Vision of Democracy and Communism

In the United States and elsewhere, the battle in civil society means that in the long term we will have to openly debate and win over broad sectors of the populace to socialism, and even communism, as the alternative to capitalism. Today revolutionary movements, before they can seize political power, will have to put down deep roots in the entire society, changing its values and its ideology. This means that the ideology of the new society will have already sprouted even before the final victory. Just as the feudal system was penetrated from within by capitalism, so also will capitalism be undermined from within by socialist and communist ideas.

Democratic values will form an integral part of the broader struggle for building the communist society that Karl Marx enunciated in the *Communist Manifesto* over a century ago. Like Marx, we today are still struggling for an end to the exploitation of man by his fellow man, for an end to alienation, and for an end to private property, the state, and the traditional concept of the monogamous and patriarchal family. Part and parcel of this struggle is our right as revolutionaries to reflect on and discuss our ideas freely, to tell the world openly who we are and to fight to transform that same world without hypocrisy. We are in favor of decentralization, collectivization, and the democratization and humanization of the family. In the new society the individual beliefs of everyone must be respected. One can be a Christian, an Atheist, a Jew or a Moslem. These beliefs are an individual matter. We should only oppose religions or beliefs that try to impose themselves on others. If, on the other hand, we were to set ourselves up as the infallible vanguard and to impose our vision on society by force, we would end by losing power before ever having conquered it, just as so many radical movements have in the past.

In a socialist society, there must also be a great deal of leeway for individuals and groups to pursue their own particular interests. Marx said that under communism one should be able to work and to go fishing when one wanted. This may be an ideal formulation of communism, but it does reflect the need for flexibility in a communist society so that everyone can pursue their productive and creative interests. Personal or 'private enterprise' on a small scale is desirable component of a communist society. Many will want to run their own artisan enterprises, their own restaurants, their book stores, their recreation facilities, and so on. Macro-economic objectives and large scale enterprises will have to be created and run by society as a whole. But this does not mean that the spirit of enterprise on the individual level should be repressed. Democratic socialism means not only the right to participate in determining the direction of society, but perhaps even more importantly the right to choose what one wants to do with one's life. Ultimately, this is what communism is all about – the complete liberation of the individual to pursue personal interests that rebound to the benefit of the entire society.

The Coming Battles

Certainly the final stronghold of capitalism in the Western Hemisphere will be in the United States. But it will be simultaneously besieged from within and without. Large sectors of the US population – whites, Blacks, Latinos, workers, and sectors of the middle class will turn against the capitalist-imperialist order and all the destructive tendencies that it represents. Revolutions to the south will certainly influence the process, especially as the fourth force grows in importance within the United States. But just as important will be the demands, needs and interests of broad sectors of the US population that come up against the narrow self-interests of the ruling classes.

The political revolution has already begun in the Americas. It is not simply that Cuba and Nicaragua have crossed the threshold into the post-capitalist era. What really announces the advent of the political revolution is the new social, economic and political upheaval that reverberates across the hemisphere. The urban guerrillas in Chile, the awakening popular movement in the villages of Haiti, the advanced state of social mobilization in Peru, the militant movement of workers and radical Catholics in Brazil, the liberated zones in El Salvador, the emergent unity on the Mexican left, and the solidarity movements and the Rainbow Coalition in the United States: these are the signs that the 1990s will be the era of a New Left, democratic and internationalist, in the Americas.

Notes

Introduction

1. Regis Debray, *Revolution in the Revolution*, New York 1969.
2. Carlos Marighella, *Minimanual para la guerrilla urbana*, Mexico D.F. 1968.
3. See the exemplary discussion in Richard Fagen, Carmen Deere, and Jose Luis Coraggio, *Transition and Development: Problems in Third World Socialism*, Monthly Review/CENSA, New York 1986; also Paul Sweezy, *Post-Revolutionary Society*, Monthly Review, New York 1980.
4. See Orlando Núñez, 'The Political Conditions of the Transition', in Fagen, et. al.
5. For an introduction to the contemporary revolutionary movements in Latin America, see Pablo González Casanova, *Imperialismo y Liberación*, Mexico D.F. 1968.

Chapter 1

1. José Carlos Mariátegui, *Seven Interpretative Essays on Peruvian Reality*, translated by Marjory Urquidi, Austin 1971. Also see Harry E. Vanden, *National Marxism in Latin America: José Carlos Mariátegui's Thought and Politics*, Boulder 1986; and Roberto Paris, 'La formacion ideologica de José Carlos Mariátegui', *Cuadernos de Pasado y Presente*, 92, Mexico D.F. 1981.
2. See Márta Harnecker, *Del moncada a la victoria (La strategia politica de Fidel)*, Instituto de Investigaciones, Cambio y Desarrollo, Lima 1985.
3. For a contemporary discussion of the Unidad Popular in Chile see Lelio Basso, Rossana Rossanda, Márta Harnecker, et al., *Transición al socialismo y experiencia Chilena*, Santiago 1972. A later balance-sheet is Sergio Bitar, *Transición, socialismo y democracia: la experiencia Chilena*, Mexico 1979.
4. For an analysis of how capitalist development has affected political processes in Central America see Roger Burbach and Patricia Flynn, *Agribusiness in the Americas*, Monthly Review Press, New York 1980.
5. William Appleman Williams, *The Tragedy of American Diplomacy*, New

York 1962; and Harry Magdoff, *The Age of Imperialism*, Monthly Review Press, New York 1968.

6. Paul Sweezy, *The Theory of Capitalist Development*, New York 1942.

7. Paul Baran, *The Political Economy of Growth*, Monthly Review Press, New York 1957.

8. André Gunder Frank, *Capitalismo y subdesarrollo en América Latina*, Mexico 1978 (6th edition).

9. Theotonio Dos Santos, 'La crisis de la teoria del desarrollo y las relaciones de dependencia en America Latina', *Cuadernos de estudios socio-económicos*, 11, Universidad de Chile 1970; and Ruy Mauro Marini, *Subdesarrollo y revolución*, Mexico 1969.

10. Ernesto Che Guevara de la Serna, *Obras, 1957–62*, Volume 2. Casa de las Americas, La Habana, Cuba 1970, p. 92.

Chapter 2

1. See Roger Burbach and Patricia Flynn, *The Politics of Intervention: The United States in Central America*, Monthly Review/CENSA, New York 1984; and Bill Robinson and Kent Norsworthy, *David and Goliath: The US War Against Nicaragua*, Monthly Review/CENSA, New York 1986.

2. *The Report of the National Bipartisan Commission on Central America*, New York 1984.

3. See Hal Draper, *Karl Marx and Frederic Engels: Writing on the Paris Commune*, Monthly Review Press, New York 1971, p. 130.

4. Carole Bengelsdorf, 'State and Society in the Transition to Socialism' in Fagen et al.

5. For an example of the new revisionism which proposes to discard Marxism, see Samuel Bowles and Herbert Gintis, *Democracy and Capitalism: Property, Community and the Contradictions of Modern Social Thought*, New York 1986.

6. Jaime Wheelock Roman, *Habla la vanguardia*, DAP-FSLN, Managua 1981.

7. Carlos M. Vilas, *La revolución sandinista; liberación nacional y transformaciones sociales en Centroamérica*, Buenos Aires 1984.

8. Bayardo Arce, Humberto Ortega and Jaime Wheelock, *Sandinistas*, Editorial Vanguardia, Managua 1984.

9. Centro de Investigaciones y Estudios de la Reforma Agraria, *La democracia participativa en Nicaragua*, CIERA, Managua 1984.

10. Orlando Núñez, *Luttes de classes au Nicaragua*, PhD Thesis, Paris 1986.

11. For a debate on socialism and democracy, see James Petras, 'Authoritarianism, Democracy and the Transition to Socialism' in *Socialism and Democracy: The Bulletin of the Research Group on Socialism and Democracy* 1; Peter Roman, 'A Critical Response to Petras', ibid.

Chapter 3

1. See *Conferencia teórica internacional. Características generales y particulares de los procesos revolucionarios en America Latina y el Caribe, Memorias*, La Habana, 26–28 April 1982.

2. See Orlando Núñez, 'Las fuerzas clasistas de la revolución popular sandinista' in *Cuadernos de sociologia* 2, Escuela de Sociologia, Universidad Centroamericana de Nicaragua, Managua 1986.

3. Orlando Núñez, 'La tercera fuerza en los movimientos de liberación nacional' in *Las fuerzas clasistas*, op cit.

4. See Carlos Marin, 'Costa Rica: Las luchas sociales en un período de crisis', *Revista de ciencias sociales*, 30, CSUCA, San Jose 1985, pp. 97–113.

5. For the political analyses of the left since the coup, see Fernández Gilberto, *Dictadura militar y oposición política en Chile*, 1973–1981, CEDLA, Amsterdam 1985.

6. See Carlos Iván De Gregorio, *Sendero Luminoso: una breve historia*, Instituto de Estudios Peruanos, Lima 1985.

7. See Joaquin Villalobos, 'El estado actual de la guerra y sus perspectivas', *Estudios Centroamericanos*, San Salvador, May 1986.

Chapter 4

1. See 'The Cuban Crisis and the Peace Movement' in *Common Sense* IV,2, New York, 1 December 1962.

2. The most comprehensive, although partisan, account is Fred Halstead, *Out Now: A Participant's Account of the American Movement Against the Vietnam War*, New York 1978.

3. For an evocation of this 'neo-Bolivarism', see Bayardo Arce, *Nicaragua Sandinista ante la crisis internacional (Discurso de clausura ante el primer congreso del pensamiento anti-imperialista)*, Managua, February 1985.

4. See Roger Burbach and Marc Herold, 'The US Stake in the Caribbean Basin' in *The Politics of Intervention*, op. cit.

5. For a survey of the polls, see William Leo Grande, *Central America and the Polls*, Washington Office on Latin America, Washington D.C. 1984.

6. This conception is being actively developed by the Policy Alternatives for Caribbean and Central America (PACCA) whose *An Alternative Future for Central America* is forthcoming.